TRACING YOUR TRADE AND CRAFTSMEN ANCESTORS

FAMILY HISTORY FROM PEN & SWORD

TRACING YOUR TRADE AND CRAFTSMEN ANCESTORS

A Guide for Family Historians

Adèle Emm

Pen & Sword
FAMILY HISTORY

Dedication
For Pasqualle

*

First published in Great Britain in 2015
PEN & SWORD FAMILY HISTORY
an imprint of
Pen & Sword Books Ltd
47 Church Street
Barnsley, South Yorkshire, S70 2AS

ISBN 978 1 47382 362 4

A CIP catalogue record for this book is
available from the British Library.

Typeset in Palatino and Optima by CHIC GRAPHICS

Printed and bound in England by
CPI Group (UK), Croydon, CR0 4YY

Pen & Sword Books Ltd incorporates the imprints of Pen & Sword
Archaeology, Atlas, Aviation, Battleground, Discovery, Family History,
History, Maritime, Military, Naval, Politics, Railways, Select, Social History,
Transport, True Crime, Claymore Press, Frontline Books, Leo Cooper,
Praetorian Press, Remember When, Seaforth Publishing and Wharncliffe.

For a complete list of Pen & Sword titles please contact
PEN & SWORD BOOKS LTD
47 Church Street, Barnsley, South Yorkshire, S70 2AS, England
E-mail: enquiries@pen-and-sword.co.uk
Website: www.pen-and-sword.co.uk

CONTENTS

Contents

PREFACE

I started researching my family history at seventeen when I wondered where my silly (as I then thought) surname came from. In those days, decades before www.freebmd.org and online census records, you pulled down large, red tomes of birth, marriage and death registers from shelves in St Catherine's House. Many of my forebears were agricultural labourers but, sprinkled liberally throughout, were butchers, bakers, shoemakers, coal merchants, drapers and ironmongers, some of whom made vast sums of money and retired to the suburbs, whilst others scraped a living into their seventies.

We all have someone in our family history who followed similar occupations; the butcher, baker, and candlestick-maker of nursery rhyme fame. This book is about their life, training and working conditions, as well as how to flesh out their lives from records, many of which are sparse and difficult to locate. People with money or lineage left records behind, but those living a hand-to-mouth existence following a trade or craft often didn't and therein lies the fun of the chase. Finding their name is exciting. Seeing their signature, as I did for my great-great-grandfather in an auctioneers' 1838 account book is wondrous. A year later, aged thirty-eight, he was dead from 'inflammation of the brain,' possibly meningitis, an illness which could carry us off even now. A bittersweet revelation.

Websites were correct at the time of writing. Either the photos came from family albums, for which I thank my ancestors, hoarders like myself, or I took them. The copyright remains with me. I must thank Nan Cawthorne, a fellow Emm and as indefatigable an Emm chaser as myself.

ACKNOWLEDGEMENTS

David Beasley, Librarian, Worshipful Company of Goldsmiths

Cambridgeshire Archives for permission to reproduce their archives

Katie Cavanagh, Stockport Hat Works. Photos of planking kettle, hatter's bow and hatters' blocks courtesy of the Stockport Hat Works and Stockport Metropolitan Museum

Nancy Cawthorne for her knowledge of the saddle and harness industry and fabulous suggestions

Simon Grant-Jones, blacksmith

Dr Miles Lambert, Senior Curator, Gallery of Costume, Manchester Art Gallery

The National Archives and British Library for researching and answering my strange questions

Geraint Parfitt, clogmaker

Rebecca Shawcross, Shoe Resources Officer, Northampton Museums and Art Gallery, for reading and revising Chapter 8. Any mistakes are mine

Robert Spurrett for reading through the manuscript and helpful suggestions.

Chapter 1
INTRODUCTION TO TRADE AND CRAFTS

Tinker, tailor, soldier sailor,
Rich man, poor man, beggar man, thief.
(Traditional counting game)

The memory of our forebears' occupations lingers on in surnames: Butcher, Baker, Thatcher, Potter, Carpenter, Smith, Cooper, Tailor et al are common not only in English, but also elsewhere. Bäcker (baker), Schmidt (smith), Schneider (tailor) in German; Fournier (man of the oven), Boulanger (baker), Lefevre (iron smith) and Chevalier (knight) in France. Tailor has an equivalent in over twenty languages, to name a few: Krawiec/Kravitz in Polish, Darzi in Hindi and Urdu, Kleermaker in Dutch and Sastre in Spanish. Some surnames refer to trades and crafts which no longer exist: Tozer from combing and carding wool and Walker from fulling (cleaning wool for clothmaking). Occupational surnames appear in the fifty most common UK surnames as compiled by Dr Muhammad Adnam and Alistair Leak of University College London from the 2007 Electoral Register. Smith is first, Taylor (Tailor) fifth, Walker and Wright twelfth and thirteenth respectively.

Most, if not all of us, have a trade or craftsman in our ancestry. In medieval times, John might be identified by his occupation; John the carpenter distinguishes him from John the potter or John the thatcher. This was important in the rise of medieval bureaucracy when for centuries John, William and Richard were the three most popular male Christian names, closely followed by Robert and

1

Thomas. If your surname is Smith, it is unlikely you will ever discover the original bearer of the name – a Plymouth smith in 1300 would be unrelated to a Paisley counterpart although working conditions would be similar.

Medieval names were fluid. As a journeyman journeyed, his 'surname' could change from his occupation to where he originated; John Baker became John of Norwich. A man's son might not have the same surname as his father, but by 1400, however, a surname was largely hereditary: your father's surname was yours too. For anyone interested in where a surname was most prolific in the 1881 census, Public Profiler on the internet (based at University College London) **www.publicprofiler.org** gives the whereabouts of all but the most uncommon surnames. Steve Archer's *Surname Atlas* on CD includes them all.

Street names also reflect trade and crafts. Bread Street, mentioned in London as early as 1302, was a bread market. Ironmonger Lane has existed in the City of London since the twelfth century. Also in the City are Milk Street and Pudding Lane, infamous as the source of the Great Fire of London in September 1666 and responsible for the destruction of virtually every guildhall in the City. What the Great Fire didn't get, the 1940 Blitz probably did. Incidentally, a 'simple clock maker' was hanged for starting the fire. The Monument, built as a permanent memorial to the fire and designed by Sir Christopher Wren and Dr Robert Hooke, rises from the corner of Monument Street and Fish Street Hill. At 202 feet high (61 meters), it is the exact distance from the source of the fire, can still be visited and, for the energetic, climbed. Good luck: there are 311 steps. Gold Streets are found in Northampton, Luddesdown (Kent), Wellingborough, Southsea and Barnsley. Other names relating to craftsmen are common, for instance Cooper's Bottom in Longbridge Deverill, Wiltshire. For trade, the Haymarket in London is where hay and straw were sold in the seventeenth century.

The importance of trade and craft is reflected in nursery rhymes, such as:

Rub a dub dub three men in a tub
And who do you think they are?
The butcher, the baker, the candlestick maker...

Bakers are mentioned vicariously in *Hot Cross Buns* and *Do you know the muffin man who lives down Drury Lane?* The muffin man rang a bell and ported a tray on his head. An early reference to muffin sellers appears in *Poor Robin's Almanac*, from 1733, and the rhyme is thought to date from around 1820 from a handwritten manuscript in the Bodleian Library, Oxford. Jane Austen's *Persuasion*, written in 1818 and pre-dating the Bodleian manuscript, mentions muffin men in Chapter Fourteen. *Molly Malone* sells her mussels in Dublin's fair city. *Hot Cross Buns* is based on a street cry.

Common expressions refer to past trades. 'Jack of all trades, master of none' is self-explanatory and regarded as derogatory today. 'Jack' was the ubiquitous medieval name (a pet name for John), albeit slightly disparaging, but integral to occupations like lumberjack, steeplejack and, indeed, the ordinary seaman, Jack Tar. Jack is used in tools: the bootjack, the jack-file, the jack-screw (and the jackboot beloved by Nazis). 'Putting your best foot forward' or the military 'From the left, quick march' refer to a man's left foot being larger than his right. For women, the right foot is usually larger than their left. In the good old days, shoe shops measured both feet, presenting the right shoe first to women and the left to men. Early shoes (like snow boots and cheap slippers) didn't distinguish between right and left, but eventually shoemakers recognised this and cut lasts and shoes accordingly.

A common feature from Victorian and Edwardian eras was that the aristocracy and professional classes looked down on people who made money 'in trade'. *Nouveau riche* has similar connotations today. This snobbery insinuated itself into public schools – Eton, Harrow and Rugby educated sons of nobility and *gentlemen*, whereas minor public schools taught sons of manufacturers, mill owners and the rest. Rev Nathaniel Woodard (1811–91), founder of eleven schools and author of *A Plea for the Middle Classes*(**https://archive.**

3

org/details/pleaformiddlecla00wood) advocated three social classes needing education as well as 'gentlemen' catered for in top public schools; 'gentlemen with small incomes, solicitors, surgeons, unbeneficed clergy and naval and military officers: respectable tradesfolk and second-rate retail shops, publicans, gin-palace keepers'.

So why were tradesmen regarded as inferior? Trade was barter in Neolithic times. You can almost hear a caveman saying, 'I have two deer and only need one. You've got a basket of berries. I'll swap a venison leg for some fruit.' Trade is the business of buying and selling goods. Alternatively, it is the purchase of raw materials and, in common parlance, giving it 'added value'. A shoemaker purchases leather to make into shoes, selling them at a higher price than the original hide. This is the craftsman. A tradesman could be as lofty as a mill owner or as lowly as a pedlar…

Working in trade could be lucrative. Joseph Emm (1814–87), a servant at his marriage in 1847 and the son of a servant, according to his marriage certificate, ran the Black Horse in Wood Street, Chipping Barnet, for over twenty years. By 1881, his son Arthur ran it, although Joseph was still listed as proprietor in Kelly's 1886 directory. By 1891, Arthur lived on independent means in Barnet and is described as 'gentleman' at his daughter's wedding in 1906. Whether or not the locals agreed is immaterial; in 1903, he left his widow over £5,600. This figure pales into insignificance against the probate of Louisa Ann Martin (1860–1924), a school teacher before her marriage who, after running a public house in Rochdale, left a staggering £13,300 in 1924, enough for all her surviving siblings to buy a house outright. Trade may have been 'looked down upon' but it was 'up there' as far as money was concerned.

It is important to note that the Establishment, gentry and polite society, were largely Anglican, whereas *nouveau riche* entrepreneurs, industrialists and working-class folk were commonly Nonconformist – indeed, professions such as medicine and law were barred to Dissenters. Louisa Ann Martin hailed from a Nonconformist family who, although they condemned the 'demon drink', weren't averse to selling it. You only need look at the religious breakdown of towns like Olney and Newport Pagnell in 1600s Buckinghamshire to find that a large proportion of the population were chapel not church, even when not attending church was a criminal offence. Tradesmen ancestors may well be in Nonconformist records.

A craftsman is a skilled manual worker making functional and/or decorative objects; shoes and horse harnesses are both functional and attractive.

Effectively, tradesmen and craftsmen, no matter how wealthy, were shunned as inferior because, basically, they were not gentlemen.

Das Ständebuch (The Book of Trades) was published in 1586 in Germany and features different trades, sycophantically opening with 'king'. Several English versions of *The Book of Trades or Library of Useful Arts* from 1806 (free online via Google books) define the trades of woolcomber, spinner, waterman, basket maker, hat maker, jeweller, bricklayer, carpenter, cooper, stonemason, sawyer, smith, shipwright, mariner, currier, apothecary, baker, straw hat maker, soap boiler, plumber, dyer, potter and type-founder, with an illustration for each and description of skills, tools, job and pay. Many might now be classified as craft rather than trade, but the term is often synonymous. An 1818 edition with more trades is found at **https://archive.org/stream/bookenglishtrad00soutgoog**.

The 1806 version outlines, for instance, how much a journeyman cooper earned, what they produced, and the method and tools required. The entry for stonemason explains types of marble, how it is treated, how much he and his labourer might earn and the fact they are piece workers. This Georgian careers advice manual explains which trades were the more skilful and profitable, which had fewer practitioners and who charged what.

Modern life has been influenced by the economic stability of Elizabeth I's reign (1558–1603), during which luxury goods were imported from around the known world. During her reign, the London stock exchange was financed and set up by Sir Thomas Gresham (1519–79). In 1543, he became a liveryman of the Mercers'

London Royal Exchange c.1906, showing inset the weathervane in the form of Gresham's symbol, the grasshopper. (Author's collection, ©Adèle Emm)

Company, importing goods from the Low Countries, mostly Belgium and the Netherlands. In 1565 he set up a *bourse*, or exchange, at his own expense. In order to do so, he negotiated with the Aldermen of London for the purchase of a suitable piece of land on which to build. Although the land is still owned by the City of London Corporation and the Worshipful Company of Mercers, the original building burnt down in the Great Fire of London. His emblem, the grasshopper, can still be seen on the weathervane at the Royal Exchange and on the coat of arms for Gresham College, founded in 1597 from his bequests.

The Industrial Revolution saw a proliferation in trade and craftsmen alongside a huge population rise. In 1801, the population in Britain was 15.6 million. By 1861, it had reached 27.8 million. More people meant more demand for clothing, shoes, housing, tools and food. The British Empire was building railways in India with Britain supplying the equipment. This was a chance for everyone to get in on the act.

Unfortunately, 1870s England was hit by a massive slump, which gravely affected the lives of everyone, especially agricultural labourers. Working a ten and a half hour day, a farm labourer in Devon might pull in seven shillings a week: not enough to support a family. According to *The Book of Trades* a journeyman mason in 1806 could earn over twenty-four shillings a week. It made sense to train children for a trade.

Occupation Records

Occupations are discovered in a variety of ways. The parish registers date from 1538 when, after Henry VIII's split from Rome, Thomas Cromwell ordered all parishes to keep a book recording baptism, marriages and burials of the parishioners for the previous week. Some regarded the directive as a precursor to a tax and resisted it. Many books were lost during the chaos of the English Civil War (1643–47) or in later years – four hundred years is a long time. The registers were kept in a locked coffer and subject to mould, moths and other threats. From 1598, entries were copied and sent to the Diocese Office and these copies, known as the *Bishop's Transcripts*, are often the only copies in existence. Needless to say, copying incurred errors. In 1603, in order to pay for the books, a law was passed whereby the parish paid a tax for each entry so, inevitably, some weren't entered. By 1706, after many revisions of the charges, the tax was abolished. By 1711, books were ruled, numbered and, from 1733, written in English not Latin. Whether or not the parish records complied with the rules depended on the vicar. In 1751–52, the calendar changed from Julian to Gregorian and eleven days were 'lost'. At the same time, the year changed to start on 1 January and not Lady Day, 25 March. Effectively, anyone born from January to the end of March was born in what we now regard as the previous year.

The earliest baptism registers give only the baby and its father's names. Later, they record the name of the mother as well e.g. Brown, Rbt son of Wm and Matilda. From 1813, baptism registers for legitimate births recorded the occupation of the father, although I have seen them earlier; in Bampton, Oxfordshire, they appear sporadically from 1695. For illegitimate children, of course, there may be no father's name, although some vicars named putative fathers. No occupation has been recorded for any I've seen. If your ancestors were in Yorkshire circa 1770 to 1813, you may strike lucky and find family names in the Dade registers, named after William Dade, a Yorkshire clergyman. In these, information is given about parents and often grandparents of the child being baptised.

The Marriage Act of 1753 meant all women under twenty-one required parental or guardian consent. This was to prevent the proliferation of illegal marriages in which wealthy men married underage girls (many of these marriages were bigamous) and where a marriage could take place anywhere in the country as long as a vicar officiated. If a clergyman ignored the law, he could be transported for fourteen years! In 1754, the register of marriages was recorded in a different book to births and soon there was a pre-printed template for marriages. Records of banns had to be kept and many records are still in existence.

In 1929, the age of marriage was raised to sixteen for both sexes in the Ages of Marriages Act. It had previously been fourteen for boys and twelve for girls, although it's rare to find brides and grooms this young and anyone under twenty-one needed parental consent anyway.

By the middle of the eighteenth century, the occupation of the groom was recorded on the pre-printed form on the marriage register, but not the name or occupation of the father. By civil registration in 1837, the printed registration form had a column for 'rank or profession' for bride, groom and their fathers. If the father of the bride or groom had died, the registration form might record 'dec'd'. The bride's column was often empty. Remember, too, that the happy couple's description of their fathers' occupations could be embellished or inflated.

Death certificates also give the rank, profession and trade of the deceased person. Again, mistakes occur and these are not necessarily intentional. Dates of birth for early civil registrations can be inaccurate simply because someone was unsure of when they were born.

Wills and probate may record the profession of the testator, but not always. James Carter, who died in Fakenham, Norfolk, in January 1858, is described as a dealer in skins leaving effects worth under £50. If you are lucky, the will might list the testator's premises, tools and other objects of worth. Women are usually described as wife, widow or spinster and her occupation may not be mentioned unless she was single. Until 1882, a married woman couldn't hold property in her own right so she couldn't make a will without the approval of her husband and, as he owned everything anyway, it was a pointless exercise. A widow or spinster might wish to state where her assets were to go after death. For wills and probate which state the deceased's occupation, fascinating detail can be supplied, especially in inventories describing chattels, such as tools, clothing and accommodation. The inventory of an ancestor of mine who died in 1701, admittedly not a trade or craftsman, was incredibly detailed, itemising crops in each field and all his furniture and clothing. The total valuation? £388 1d. Occupations are often recorded in wills after 1858. Responsibility for proving wills prior to 11 January 1858 was with the ecclesiastical authorities. After this, the Principal Probate Registry was responsible and records can be found online on genealogical websites such as Ancestry and FindMyPast. Origins, now subsumed into FindMyPast, has the fifty-four York Peculiars Probate on its National Wills Index, which includes over 25,000 wills and probate documents from 1383 to 1857. These have the testator's first and last name, occupation, places associated with them and date.

Local wills can be accessed free in public libraries and county record offices. For more information about wills, including an extensive appendix of sources for all the counties and pre-1858 probate courts in England and Wales, refer to the excellent *The Wills of our Ancestors* by Stuart A. Raymond, Pen and Sword, 2012.

Another source of occupations is the loyalty oath rolls of 1723. These listed everyone over eighteen who would swear loyalty to the monarch during a perceived papist threat. Not all counties' records exist but those that do (plus further information) has been compiled by Edward Vallance of Roehampton University and is found on **www.historyworkingpapers.org/?page_id=373**. You must visit the relevant archives to view the Rolls. The Society of Genealogists (SoG) holds a transcription of the City of London Rolls. Only the Devonshire Rolls have been fully indexed.

Court cases reported in either court minutes or a newspaper often mention a profession or trade. From the Central Criminal Court minutes for the 1835 trial of Thomas Fisher (aged eleven!) we learn that John Emm is a ladies' shoemaker and that the prisoner, Thomas Fisher, was apprenticed to him on the previous 28 January. Old Bailey Online is excellent, with minutes published free at **www.oldbaileyonline.org**. There is a useful search engine and some defendants, witnesses, victims and convicts originated from outside London.

Censuses record a person's 'profession, trade, employment or of independent means' from 1841 onwards. Remember that although many women in poorer households worked to keep the wolf from the door, this may not have been reported to the enumerator. On the other hand, many did report their jobs and lace makers, straw plaiters and others feature highly in areas where such cottage industries were common. In fact, a research project by the University of Essex in 2014 showed that many women were the main breadwinners between 1851 and 1901, particularly in the working classes. We genealogists knew this already… You may also find that the daughter of say, a shoemaker, worked for her father as a binder (see Chapter 8). The numbers working at different trades for the 1851, 1861 and 1871 census records can be found on **www.**

victorianweb.org/history/census.html. For the 1831 and later census breakdowns, refer to the Online Historical Population Reports (OHPR) at www.histpop.org.

From 1901 the census has a column for 'employer, worker or own account' with the neighbouring column stating if the person is 'working at home'. The 1911 has four columns relating to 'PROFESSION or OCCUPATION of Persons aged ten years and upwards' and includes personal occupation, the industry or service to which they are connected, if they are working on their own account or employed and finally whether they are working at home.

A common problem is deciphering the actual job stated in the census. Many occupations prior to the 1830s are now obsolete. The same occurs in reverse. A useful website to help with this is http://homepage.ntlworld.com/hitch/gendocs/trades.html outlining the ranks, professions, occupations and trades, giving a one-line definition of jobs listed in the censuses. It is also useful for ranks or professions listed on birth and marriage certificates. You could also try www.rmhh.co.uk/occup. The Oxford English Dictionary is helpful in deciphering professions and trade but is an expensive subscription; however, it is accessible free at any local library with an account.

Workhouse admission and desertion records, where they still exist, state occupation. Deserters might have their physical description published in the *Poor Law Gazette*. The settlement examination system may provide information about occupations. As poor relief was only given to a family from that parish, it was common for people to be moved around the country and returned to their parish of origin. These records are useful for the poorer members of society such as itinerant craftsmen; examination records, settlement certificates and removal orders and other Poor Law records are held at local record offices and the information contains birthplace, age and occupation. Also try Discovery at The National Archives.

Other resources recording occupations are emigration records. The passenger lists for ships sailing to America, for instance, list age, profession, occupation/calling of adult passengers and in many cases a UK address, which class they are sailing and whether or not they intend to make the destination their future home. Online genealogy services have these and Peter Christian's book, *The Genealogist's Internet*, gives helpful advice for tracking emigration around the world. With a quick Google search and armed with the name of the ship, you may find a photograph of the very vessel plus further details.

If you are fortunate enough to count a distinguished person among your forebears, they may be commemorated by a blue plaque, statue or other monument. Originally initiated by the Royal Society of Arts in 1866, the blue plaque scheme transferred to the London County Council in 1901 and, on its abolition, to the Greater London Council (GLC). Since 1986, the scheme has been under the auspices of English Heritage. *Lived in London: Blue Plaques and the Stories Behind Them*, edited by Emily Cole, published jointly by English Heritage and Yale University Press, tells the stories behind the plaques. At the time of writing, there were 880 official blue plaques in London. Other cities and towns such as Manchester and Rochdale run similar schemes. A Google search identifies maps to the plaques.

A quirky website **www.londonremembers.com** is a fun attempt to photograph and 'archive' all the plaques and memorials in London. Unless you have a celebrated ancestor it may not be of any interest other than entertainment. For statues and memorials elsewhere in the country which may throw up occupational information for the family historian, you may have to resort to a Google search; **www.manchester2002-uk.com/buildings/statues** lists statues, dates of erection and location for statues and monuments in Manchester and surrounding districts and local tourism sites may help. Of course, the reason you are pursuing a hobby in family history means you have not yet discovered a famous forebear, but if you do, visiting the plaques and monuments is a welcome bonus.

Chapter 2
GUILDS

You may scold a carpenter who has made you a bad table,
though you cannot make a table.
It is not your trade to make tables.
Dr Samuel Johnson, (1709–84)

From the early Middle Ages, guilds were incredibly powerful and important. *Gild*, deriving from Middle English and Old Norse, means gold or payment. Anyone wishing to trade in a town or city had to belong to a guild, effectively ensuring good practice and, as we would say today, 'quality control'. Guilds controlled the number of members and regulated wages, working conditions and trading. Medieval guilds were a monopoly, although their influence had waned by the seventeenth century.

There were two types of guild, merchant and craft, which became virtually indistinguishable over the years. The medieval like-minded merchants travelled together to protect against brigands, and trade guilds were artisans pursuing the same occupation e.g. cutlers, bakers and butchers.

There are still 110 guilds in London today. Livery Companies were named after the ornate uniform (livery) worn in the Middle Ages, now known as 'Worshipful Company of…' or 'Company of…' Those founded after 1709 (e.g. Fanmakers) are Modern Livery Companies and include some twentieth-century companies, such as Actuaries and Insurers.

No one could trade in a city governed by guilds unless they were a member – a freeman – bound by their ordinances (rules). Should a freeman transgress any ordinance by, for instance, selling underweight goods, sanctions were severe and recorded; good evidence for the family historian. Although most freemen belonged to the guild relevant to their trade, it wasn't mandatory, so a mercer, for instance, could and quite often did belong to another Company.

The rules for joining a guild were strict; the most common way was to complete an apprenticeship under a guild member. From the 1750s, there were other ways; *patrimony* if your father was a member, or the rarer method, *redemption*, buying one's way in. Some records still survive. By the seventeenth century, however, the power of the guilds had disintegrated and after 1800 it was unlikely for a shoemaker, for instance, to belong to any Company, although apprenticeships were still the accepted method of training until well into the twentieth century.

Once an apprentice had completed his apprenticeship, he became a *journeyman*, qualified in his trade but too inexperienced to trade on his own, therefore generally working under a *master*. For further information about apprenticeships, see Chapter 3.

Many towns and cities outside London had guilds; Shrewsbury, Grimsby, Durham, York, Luton, Richmond (Yorkshire) and Oxford, among others. In their 1415 heyday, ninety-six trade guilds flourished in York, largely losing their influence by the late sixteenth century.

After founding, a Company built a hall in which to meet, keep records, coordinate business matters and act as warehouse for products or provisions, such as coal in case of shortages. Unfortunately, virtually all medieval London halls (Mercers, Butchers, Coopers, Skinners, Vintners and more) were destroyed during the Great Fire of London in 1666 and many replacements came to a sticky end either in another fire (the Saddlers for example) or during the 1940 Second World War Blitz. The Ironmongers Hall, which has been on its current site since 1922, escaped the Great Fire but was hit by a German bomb during the First World War. Often, the only way to visit these halls is via private functions and weddings, as explained on their websites. Sightseeing from the street is free.

The Ironmongers' Hall has been on this site since 1922. The first hall was destroyed in the Great Fire in 1666 and a German bomb in the First World War destroyed a later one. (©Adèle Emm)

Some Companies display their treasure, regalia and other paraphernalia at their hall, often inaccessible to the general public apart from online. The occasional public exhibition is held for special events such as the 350th anniversary of the Needlemakers' Royal Charter in 2014.

The Great Twelve Livery Companies

In 1515, the forty-eight London Livery Companies were placed in order of precedence based on power or financial status. In other words, wealthier guilds bought their way to a higher position. The precedence was important; the position in ceremonial processions depended on the order; the higher the precedence, the nearer the front of the procession. The top twelve became known as the Great Twelve City Livery Companies and most were merchants' guilds. According to legend, the expression 'at sixes and sevens' comes from the Skinners and Merchant Taylors (numbers six and seven) failing to agree on their order; every Easter they take turns to be number six or seven. The following is a list of the Great Twelve and, although I have dated the companies, most were in existence before their Royal Charter, some as early as 1100. Few surviving early records are relevant to family historians as they are mainly ordinances.

1. Worshipful Company of Mercers (general merchants) Royal Charter 1394 **www.mercers.co.uk**
2. Worshipful Company of Grocers; Company of Grossers from 1373–76 when its name changed to the current title **www.grocershall.co.uk**
3. Worshipful Company of Drapers (wool and cloth merchants); Royal Charter 1364 (an informal association existed from 1180) **www.thedrapers.co.uk**
4. Worshipful Company of Fishmongers; Royal Charter 1272 **www.fishhall.org.uk**
5. Worshipful Company of Goldsmiths; Royal Charter 1327 (assayed gold and silver from 1300; platinum from 1975) **www.thegoldsmiths.co.uk**

The impressive entrance to Drapers' Hall, Throgmorton Street, City of London. Third in the order of preference. Also see Chapter 5. (©Adèle Emm)

6. Worshipful Company of Merchant Taylors (tailors) alternating with the Skinners; Royal Charter 1503. The Taillourshalle, Threadneedle Street site owned since at least 1392 **www.merchant-taylors. co.uk**

7. Worshipful Company of Skinners (fur traders) alternates with Merchant Taylors; Royal Charter 1327 **www.skinners hall.co.uk**

8. Worshipful Company of Haberdashers (traders of sewing articles); first ordinances 1371, coat of arms adopted 1446; Royal Charter 1448. Joined by hat makers in 1502, not to be confused with the Company of Feltmakers (see Chapter 9) **www.haberdashers.co.uk**

9. Worshipful Company of Salters (traders of salt and chemicals); Royal Charter 1394 **www.salters.co.uk**

10. Worshipful Company of Ironmongers. Ferroners in 1300; Charter of Incorporation 1463. Grant of Arms 1455 **www. ironmongers.org**

11. Worshipful Company of Vintners (wine merchants); Royal Charter 1363 **www.vintnershall.co.uk**

12. Worshipful Company of Clothworkers. The Company of Fullers (Royal Charter 1480) and Company of Shearmen (Royal Charter 1508) amalgamated to form the Company of Clothworkers; Royal Charter 1528 **www.clothworkers.co.uk**

Tracing Guild Ancestors

Anyone who has ancestors in a London guild might find them in Guildhall Library; copies are on microfilm at London Metropolitan Archives (LMA), incorporated with Guildhall but on a different site. An overview of the type of records and date range for the worshipful companies are found in *The Guide to Greater London History Sources Volume 1, The City of London*. To find which records are held at Guildhall, refer to *City of London Livery Companies and Related Organisations, A Guide to their Archives in Guildhall Library*, in its fourth edition at the time of writing, or via the online catalogue.

For apprentices indentured in London, it is worth noting that rural families from Oxfordshire and further afield apprenticed their sons to London guilds. Cliff Webb's invaluable handy guides for each Company (Vintners, Plumbers, Masons etc), published by the Society of Genealogists (SoG), indexes and catalogues in alphabetical order the names of apprentices, father's name, occupation and location and name of the master. Many company archives are published in book format viewable both at Guildhall and SoG. Microfilm copies may be available.

Some London records (Clothworkers, Drapers, Leathersellers, Mercers, Saddlers, Salters and Stationers) are stored in their Company archives and you'll need an appointment to view them. However, ROLLCO (Records of London's Livery Companies Online) **www.londonroll.org** in partnership with the Centre for Metropolitan History is an online database for four of these: Clothworkers, Drapers, Goldsmiths and Mercers. At the time of writing, ROLLCO supplies information about apprentices for the following years:

Clothworkers' 1545–1908
Drapers' c.1400–1900
Mercers' 1339–1900
some Goldsmiths' 1600–1700 (see Chapter 7)

By keying in a surname, it is possible to discover the relevant archive (Clothworkers, Drapers etc) the date, event, role and status. This is a not-for-profit project and online results are free. Other Companies are planned.

The Northern Ireland Salters' records are held in the Public Record Office in Belfast **www.proni.gov.uk** and Discovery (formerly A2A) **http://discovery.nationalarchives.gov.uk** has a catalogue of Salters' deeds and related papers.

For those with guild ancestors outside London, seek out the relevant record office. Most of these have online catalogues although they are occasionally difficult to negotiate. Unfortunately, continuous records for many areas are no longer in existence. Taking Durham's guild records held at the university as an example, their records are mainly for the sixteenth to twentieth centuries and include charters and 'ordinaries' (ordinances, e.g. regulations), minutes, freemen's admittances, call roles, lists of freemen, apprenticeship admittances and registers, accounts, fines and miscellaneous correspondence. Most of their material is for Barbers, Masons and Mercers' Companies, but they also have archives relating to many trades and crafts mentioned in this book.

Another example is Shropshire. The Shrewsbury guild records include small collections for their Glovers' Company, Weavers and Clothiers, Mercers, Ironmongers and Goldsmiths among others. Catalogued online through Discovering Shropshire's History page, a visit is required to view the actual documents. Grimsby's archives are held by North East Lincolnshire Council at the Town Hall and consist of 12,000 boxes of documents dating back to the thirteenth century. You may strike lucky.

If your ancestors were mercers or merchants in York, you might find references to them in Maud Sellers' *The York Mercers and Merchant Adventurers 1356–1917*, published 1918 and found at **https://archive.org/details/yorkmercersmerch00mercrich**. There is a search facility. The latter end of the book has, among other records, a list of benefactors, rent roll (1641), and account rolls where people are specifically named. Many beneficiaries were not merchants; for example on page 289, 'Mrs Jane Stainton, left by will dated 9 November 1692, a house in Coppergate, now occupied by Josiah Truslowe, sadler (sic), chargeable with the following out payments, viz.: two pounds per annum to a merchants widow (not named).'

Nowadays, many guilds are associated with education and charity issues; well-known are Merchant Taylors in Liverpool, Skinners in Royal Tunbridge Wells responsible for five schools overall, and Haberdashers. Finding their guild roles diminishing, Companies also embarked on welfare issues, building almshouses for impoverished former members and for the poor. Records, if they exist, are held at local record offices, but it may be difficult to locate specific genealogical information.

More information about guilds represented in this book is found in the relevant chapters but, for interest, the following are the remaining London Companies in order of preference up to 100. Many have trade and history information on their websites, but as some were founded as recently as the late twentieth century, there may be limited genealogical information.

13. Worshipful Company of Dyers **www.dyerscompany.co.uk**

14. Worshipful Company of Brewers **www.brewershall.co.uk**

15. Worshipful Company of Leathersellers **www.leather sellers.co.uk**

16. Worshipful Company of Pewterers **www.pewterers.org. uk**

17. Worshipful Company of Barbers (and surgeons and dentists) **www.barberscompany.org**

18. Worshipful Company of Cutlers (knife, sword and cutlery makers) **www.cutlerslondon.co.uk**. The Sheffield Company of Cutlers dating from 1624 is at **www.cutlers-hallamshire. org.uk**

19. Worshipful Company of Bakers **www.bakers.co.uk**

20. Worshipful Company of Wax Chandlers (wax candle makers) **www.waxchandlers.org.uk**

21. Worshipful Company of Tallow Chandlers (tallow candle makers) **www.tallowchandlers.org**

22. Worshipful Company of Armourers and Brasiers (armour makers and brass workers) **www.armourershall.co.uk**

23. Worshipful Company of Girdlers (swordbelt and dressbelt makers) **www.girdlers.co.uk**

24. Worshipful Company of Butchers **www.butchershall.com**

25. Worshipful Company of Saddlers **www.saddlersco.co.uk**

26. Worshipful Company of Carpenters **www.thecarpenters company.co.uk**

27. Worshipful Company of Cordwainers (fine leather workers) **www.cordwainers.org**

28. Worshipful Company of Painter-Stainers **http://painters hall.co.uk**

29. Worshipful Company of Curriers (tanned leather dressers) **www.curriers.co.uk**

30. Worshipful Company of Masons **www.masonslivery.org**

31. Worshipful Company of Plumbers **www.plumbers company.org.uk**

32. Worshipful Company of Innholders **www.innholders. co.uk**

33. Worshipful Company of Founders (brass and bronze workers) **www.foundersco.org.uk**

34. Worshipful Company of Poulters (poulterers) **www. poulters.org.uk**

35. Worshipful Company of Cooks **www.cookslivery.org.uk**

36. Worshipful Company of Coopers (barrel makers) **www.coopers-hall.co.uk**

37. Worshipful Company of Tylers and Bricklayers **www.tylers andbricklayers.co.uk**

38. Worshipful Company of Bowyers (long bow makers) **www. bowyers.com**

39. Worshipful Company of Fletchers (arrow makers) **www. fletchers.org.uk**

40. Worshipful Company of Blacksmiths **http://blacksmiths company.org**

41. Worshipful Company of Joiners and Ceilers (wood craftsmen) **www.joinersandceilers.co.uk**

42. Worshipful Company of Weavers **www.weavers.org.uk**

43. Worshipful Company of Woolmen **http://woolmen.com**

44. Worshipful Company of Scriveners (court document writers and notaries public) **www.scriveners.org.uk**

45. Worshipful Company of Fruiterers **www.fruiterers.org.uk**

46. Worshipful Company of Plaisterers (plasterers) **www. plaistererslivery.co.uk**

47. Worshipful Company of Stationers and Newspaper Makers **www.stationers.org**

48. Worshipful Company of Broderers (embroiderers) **www. broderers.co.uk**

49. Worshipful Company of Upholders (upholsterers) **www.upholders.co.uk**

50. Worshipful Company of Musicians **www.wcom.org.uk**

51. Worshipful Company of Turners (lathe operators) **www.turnersco.com**

52. Worshipful Company of Basketmakers **www.basketmakersco.org**

53. Worshipful Company of Glaziers and Painters of Glass **www.worshipfulglaziers.com**

54. Worshipful Company of Horners (horn workers and plastic) **www.horners.org.uk**

55. Worshipful Company of Farriers (horseshoe makers and horse veterinarians) **www.wcf.org.uk**

56. Worshipful Company of Paviors (road and highway pavers) **http://paviors.org.uk**

57. Worshipful Company of Loriners (harness makers) **www.loriner.co.uk**

58. Worshipful Society of Apothecaries (medical practitioners and pharmacists) **www.apothecaries.org**

59. Worshipful Company of Shipwrights **www.shipwrights.co.uk**

60. Worshipful Company of Spectacle Makers **www.spectaclemakers.com**

61. Worshipful Company of Clockmakers **www.clockmakers.org**

62. Worshipful Company of Glovers **www.thegloverscompany.org**

63. Worshipful Company of Feltmakers (hat makers) **www.feltmakers.co.uk**

64. Worshipful Company of Framework Knitters **www.frameworkknitters.co.uk**

65. Worshipful Company of Needlemakers **www.needlemakers.org.uk**

66. Worshipful Company of Gardeners **www.gardenerscompany.org.uk**

67. Worshipful Company of Tin Plate Workers (wire workers) **www.tinplateworkers.co.uk**

68. Worshipful Company of Wheelwrights **www.wheelwrights.org**

69. Worshipful Company of Distillers **http://distillers.org.uk**

70. Worshipful Company of Pattenmakers (wooden shoe makers) **www.pattenmakers.co.uk**

71. Worshipful Company of Glass Sellers **www.glass-sellers.co.uk**

72. Worshipful Company of Coachmakers and Coach Harness Makers **http://coachmakers.co.uk**

73. Worshipful Company of Gunmakers **www.gunmakers.org.uk**

74. Worshipful Company of Gold and Silver Wyre Drawers (makers of thread for uniforms) **www.gswd.org.uk**

75. Worshipful Company of Makers of Playing Cards **www.makersofplayingcards.co.uk**

76. Worshipful Company of Fanmakers **www.fanmakers.com**

77. Worshipful Company of Carmen **www.thecarmen.co.uk**

78. Honourable Company of Master Mariners **www.hcmm.org.uk**

79. City of London Solicitors' Company **www.citysolicitors.org.uk**

80. Worshipful Company of Farmers **www.farmerslivery.org.uk**

81. Guild of Air Pilots and Air Navigators **www.airpilots.org**

82. Worshipful Company of Tobacco Pipe Makers and Tobacco Blenders **www.tobaccolivery.org**

83. Worshipful Company of Furniture Makers **www.furnituremkrs.co.uk**

84. Worshipful Company of Scientific Instrument Makers **www.wcsim.co.uk**

85. Worshipful Company of Chartered Surveyors **www.surveyorslivery.org.uk**

86. Worshipful Company of Chartered Accountants in England and Wales **www.wccaew.org.uk**

87. Worshipful Company of Chartered Secretaries and Administrators **www.wccsa.org.uk**

88. Worshipful Company of Builders Merchants **www.wcobm. co.uk**

89. Worshipful Company of Launderers **www.launderers. co.uk**

90. Worshipful Company of Marketors **http://marketors.org**

91. Worshipful Company of Actuaries **www.actuaries company.co.uk**

92. Worshipful Company of Insurers **www.wci.org.uk**

93. Worshipful Company of Arbitrators **www.arbitrators company.org**

94. Worshipful Company of Engineers **www.engineers company.org.uk**

95. Worshipful Company of Fuellers, founded 1605 at least **www.fuellers.co.uk**

96. Worshipful Company of Lightmongers **www.light mongers.co.uk**

97. Worshipful Company of Environmental Cleaners **http: //wc-ec.com**

98. Worshipful Company of Chartered Architects, founded 1834 **http://architects-livery-company.blogspot.co.uk**

99. Worshipful Company of Constructors **http://constructors company.org.uk**

100. Worshipful Company of Information Technologists **www.wcit.org.uk**

Chapter 3
TRAINING AND WORKING CONDITIONS

A man must serve his time to every trade
George Gordon, Lord Byron (1788–1824)

What your father did, you were likely to do too. Of course, there are exceptions, but when chasing ancestors with similar names, the person with the same occupation may be yours. Many boys were apprenticed into the same trade or craft; they knew the score, their father had the contacts but, although they often trained with their father, they could be apprenticed to another master in a different town or city.

Training and Apprenticeships

Thomas Farr, farmer and mill owner in Bassingbourn, Cambridgeshire, died in 1822. In his will, he left his estate to be kept in its entirety until his children reached twenty-one when the estate was to be sold. The proceeds were to be divided so that, among other bequests, surviving grandchildren were indentured to a trade or craft, thus ensuring their future livelihoods. The estate was administered by his son-in-law Caleb Masters who died in 1839, a year after the estate was wound up. Financed by their grandfather's legacy, his four surviving sons were indentured to a grocer, baker and draper and all did exceedingly well. Bequeathing money in wills for such a purpose was not uncommon; an apprenticeship ensured a boy had a skill for life, as protection against pauperism and penury. Just as today, education was key to prosperity.

Detail of Thomas Farr of Bassingbourn's will showing arrangements for his descendants. He died 13 December 1822. (Courtesy Cambridgeshire Archives.)

From the Middle Ages onwards, the most important training was an apprenticeship. It was usual, but not always the case, that a boy took up his apprenticeship at fourteen. It lasted as long as stipulated in the indentures, commonly seven years or until he reached twenty-one years of age, although a boy apprenticed at an older age might be apprenticed until twenty-four. After about 1800, many apprenticeships were shorter than the proverbial seven years. George Emm's apprenticeship to John Chapman of Westbury, saddle, collar and harness maker, lasted five years.

After 1601 and the poor relief system reforms, pauper and workhouse boys could be indentured from the age of seven; eight after 1834. An insurance policy against future welfare requirements, it meant someone other than the workhouse or parish relief (i.e. the taxpayers) clothed, housed and fed the boys; an apprentice lived with his master during training. Boys weren't always apprenticed out; some orphanages and workhouses trained the boys in-house, but this wasn't regarded as serving an apprenticeship as such. Here, the crafts and trades practised were 'poor' ones; husbandry, housewifery and shoemaking. Devon County Council's **www.devon.gov.uk/ apprenticeship_records** has an excellent description of the apprentice system and where to find records. If your ancestor was trained through the parish relief system, you might find details in the parish apprenticeship register. The Poor Law indexes and papers for 1836–1920 held in MH15 at the National Archives may lead you to information in the individual Poor Law unions' papers in MH12, but these mainly relate to policy and administration issues. To see them, visit the National Archives in Kew or pay someone to undertake research for you.

As the guilds' influence and hold waned, apprenticeships developed independently, but from 1563 it was a legal requirement that trades could only be practised after a serving a period of apprenticeship of seven years, and this statute remained in place until 1814. Anyone who hadn't followed an apprenticeship but was working in a trade could be taken to court and fined. The SoG has an index of approximately 1,500 private indentures dating from the seventeenth to the nineteenth centuries – *Crisp's Apprentices Indentures* which, if they survive, are at local record offices. Another SoG database, the London Apprentice Abstracts 1442 to 1850, is found at **www.origins.net** and FindMyPast (subscription required), holding about 300,000 entries on apprentices from all over the country, their parents and masters. The Board of Trade papers 1846–95, held on B19 at the National Archives, also has references to apprentices mentioned in correspondence to them.

The trial of Thomas Fisher in the Central Criminal Court, London in November 1835, from Old Bailey Online **www.oldbaileyonline. org** (version 7.0 t18351123-3), highlights apprentice conditions; 'the prisoner (Thomas Fisher) was apprenticed to my father on the 28th January last, and was eleven years old last May – he slept in the same room with me and my brother – my brother is a ladies' shoemaker – the prisoner had a separate bed.' This boy was lucky to sleep alone, especially as I suspect he came from the orphanage/workhouse where sharing was the norm even for adults (although discouraged by the authorities). Working hours were long, usually at home in a room converted to a workshop. John Emm Senior's statement explains how long; 'I was the last person up in the house; and at half-past eleven o'clock, I looked at the shutters and doors, and saw it all fast, and went to bed.' His son added, 'I went to look for the prisoner at twenty minutes to seven o'clock – it was not then light'. Thomas Fisher was found guilty of theft and sentenced to death, but recommended for mercy on account of his youth.

The apprentice's training, food, lodging and clothing were paid for under the terms of the indenture and an added stipulation was that apprentices couldn't marry. At the end of the apprenticeship, having shown enough skills at the trade, the apprentice became a journeyman. The usual practice meant he left the master who had apprenticed him, travelled to another town or village to see how business was conducted and would take on commissions working under the eye of another master until his 'masterpiece' was completed, generally after three years, when he became master in his own right. A journeyman's work was cheaper than the master's and they were paid by the day – *jour* in French – hence journeyman.

If you have lost your journeyman, try searching the area thirty to forty miles around their apprenticeship; this was about how far a man would walk to the next town. Caleb Masters Junior travelled forty miles from Bassingbourn to Newport Pagnell to work as a baker. George Emm went from Westbury to Paulton, Somerset, a similar distance.

I use the word 'him' because it was rarer for girls to be apprenticed, although relatively common for a widow to take on her husband's trade after his death or for a wife to assist in her husband's business.

Like Thomas Fisher, some apprentices ran away from their masters and details may be found in publications such as the Bath, Bristol, Gloucester and Salisbury *Journals* and the *London General Evening Post*. Some county family history societies have compiled lists of runaways extrapolated from various journals. The information given includes name, age, master's name and trade. For instance, the *Gloucester Journal* cites twenty-year-old John Broom from Lacock, Wiltshire, who ran away from Rebecca Coal, a blacksmith, in May 1755 – a good example of a woman running a business. Why did they abscond? Many apprentices were badly treated and abused and it was common to give them the nastiest, dirtiest and most dangerous jobs. Occasionally masters were brought in front of the Quarter Sessions Court and details are found in court records.

Indentures and Deeds of Apprenticeship

A lot of information can be found in indenture papers although they usually follow a template and are similar in format, containing the same obligations. George Emm's 1841 saddler indentures specify he could not: commit fornication, haunt taverns, play at cards or dice tables or get married during the period of his apprenticeship.

There was even the concept that an apprentice couldn't bring his master into disrepute; 'he shall see no damage to his said Master nor see to be done of others but to his Power shall tell or give warning to his said Master of the same.' We thought this was a modern concept.

The salary was set down in the agreement and the document signed and witnessed. Benjamin Emm, George's father, paid John Chapman £10 to train his son. George was paid a shilling a week for his first year of apprenticeship, two shillings for the second, three for his third, four for the fourth and five shillings a week in his final year – a total of 780 shillings which, at twenty shillings to the pound, meant George earned £39 by the end of his apprenticeship, £10 of

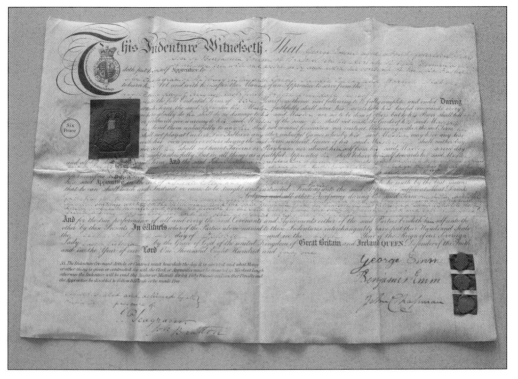

George Emm's indentures, 1841. His father, Benjamin Emm, paid John Chapman £10 to train his son Benjamin as a saddler over five years. (©Nancy Cawthorne)

which had been paid by his father. The increments show George's increasing value to his master. If we include the boy's salary, it would take just over two years to pay off his father's initial investment, although Chapman was also feeding, housing and clothing the young man. George was 'about fourteen years' when the deeds were signed.

Apprentice records, if they still exist, are found in local record offices, which usually have an online list of what they hold; the Isle of Wight holds Apprentice Indentures for Newport from 1689–1835, for instance, and the records are held by name.

In 1710 during Queen Anne's reign (1702–14) an Act of Parliament decreed that stamp duty must be paid on all indentures except where the fee was less than one shilling or had been arranged by a charity or parish. Commencing on 1 May 1710, it continued until 1804, although a few payments trickled in until January 1811. Information to circa 1750 includes name, occupation and place of origin of the father, guardian or widowed mother for more than a million named apprentices and masters. The Stamp Duty for Apprentices is held at The National Archives (IR1) and an index, the Apprentices of Great Britain 1710–74, is available on the SoG and FindMyPast websites. Images and an index for IR1 covering 1710–1811 are available on Ancestry. The SoG has microfilm of the original documents 1710–1811 and intends to complete the index to 1811 but will not be digitising them. The SoG also holds a collection of original apprenticeship indentures for 1641–1749 and 1775–1888 found on microfilm Mf 3281-3284. Some local record societies have extracted and published entries for their area.

Pay

In 1867, a statistician estimated that just over ten percent of the British population were 'higher skilled labour' earning £60 to £73 a year (between £1.15 and £1.40 a week). Forty percent of the country worked as lower skilled labourers earning £46 to £52 a year (88p – £1 a week). Farm labourers (ag labs) made up thirty per cent of the population, earning approximately £20 to £41 a year (38–79p a week). Workers in Scotland earned considerably less. To recap, the well paid skilled worker in England could earn £73 per annum, a semi-skilled worker £52 and an unskilled man £41. In Scotland, this was £68, £48 and £32 respectively, and it was less in Ireland. The worst remuneration of all was during the 1870s slump when a Highland crofter earned a pitiful £8 a year.

Compare this to salaries earned by white collar workers in the 1870s. A newly minted clerk in civil engineering earned as much as an experienced, on site engineer at about £110 a year (just over £2 a week).

Women were paid considerably less than men; the Equal Pay Act is as recent as 1970. Children, before various acts restricted the age at which they could be employed, were paid least of all and naturally many employers preferred employing women and children.

Income tax in the 1870s was four pence in the pound (less than two per cent) paid by those earning more than £150 per annum, so was unlikely to be paid by any craftsman, although a tradesman might earn that much from his business.

School Leaving Age

The Elementary Education Act 1870 established schools for children aged five to ten in England and Wales with leeway for children in agricultural areas. It was not free; parents paid thirty shillings a year per child, waived for those too poor to pay. School wasn't compulsory until the Elementary Education Act of 1880, but still wasn't free until 1891, which goes some way to explaining why a great aunt of mine born in 1879 couldn't read.

Because of the education acts, the illiteracy rate for men between 1851 and 1870 decreased from thirty-one per cent to nineteen per cent. For women, it fell from forty-five to twenty-six per cent. Practical evidence is apparent on marriage certificates, although signing a name didn't mean the person was literate – their name might be the only thing they could write. In the earlier part of Victoria's reign, a higher proportion of men signed their name while their spouse formed a cross. By the latter end of her reign, most could sign their names even in rural areas. Literacy for women largely depended on how the family felt about educating daughters. In 1802, Sarah Farr (born 1784) signed her name at her marriage in Bassingbourn, Cambridgeshire. So did all the witnesses including her sister. Her father, a miller, must have had aspirations for all his children including his daughters.

In 1893, children had to attend school until eleven and there was provision for blind and deaf children. The school leaving age was raised to twelve in 1899. In 1906, poor children received free school meals and the following year all children were medically inspected – the regime of the 'nit nurse' had begun. The Education Act of 1918 raised the school leaving age to fourteen, with part-time provision for young people up to eighteen. R.A.B. Butler raised it to fifteen in 1944; in 1972 it rose to sixteen.

Working Hours

In 1843, it was made illegal to employ children under the age of nine. Shortly afterwards, working hours for children aged nine to thirteen were reduced to forty-eight a week.

Charles Kingsley published *The Water Babies* in 1863, depicting the cruelty and degradation of children sent up chimneys. The following year, the Chimney Sweepers' Regulation Act prohibited children from climbing chimneys, although no one took any notice. The Chimney Sweepers' Act of 1875, which licensed sweeps and included police enforcement, finally halted the practice. There were estimated to be over 2,000 chimney sweeps working in London alone in the 1870s – all adults – charging six pence to three shillings to clean a chimney depending on height and locality. For extinguishing a chimney fire, a common event, a sweep could charge five shillings. A modern-day chimney sweep who retired in 2014 said that, during his sixty-five year career, he cleaned over 500,000 chimneys and, in the heyday of coal fires, his grandfather worked from 6am to 6pm cleaning up to thirty chimneys a day.

Even though children under nine were banned from working, it required the Gangs Act of 1869 to prohibit children under eight from working in itinerant gangs for stone and weed clearing, potato planting, ditch clearing and the like. Regardless of this, children as young as six were still exploited and paid a shilling a week.

The Tolpuddle Martyrs were transported from Dorset to Australia in 1843 for forming a union of agricultural workers demanding an eight-hour working day, which many of us today would relish. Fortunately for them, a petition of 250,000 names to the then Prime Minister, Lord Melbourne, meant they returned to England two years later. Tolpuddle Martyrs' Museum, Dorset, can be visited **www.tolpuddlemartyrs.org.uk**.

Pity the mill factory workers who, in the 1850s, worked seven days a week, ten hours a day Monday to Saturday with a lenient seven and a half hours on Sunday. The Factory Act 1856 ensured a factory worker finished work at 2pm on Saturdays, but they still earned a pittance.

Hours were generally long everywhere. It is well recorded that the lower the pay, the longer the hours, with seamstresses working late into the night or for as long as they could afford a candle.

My father (born 1921) remembers working in the office on Saturday mornings during the Second World War. I remember solicitors' offices being open on Saturdays as late as the 1970s, although nowadays, of course, shift patterns mean people often work weekends. After the Shops Act of 1911, shop assistants had half a day off during the week but worked a full Saturday.

Some jobs worked irregular hours; bakers, for instance, rose early in the morning to make bread overnight, finishing work in the early afternoon. It was up to those working in the shop to sell the bread itself.

The Second Sunday Observance Act 1677 banned all retail trade on Sundays except the selling of milk and food in inns, cookshops and victualling houses. The fine for breaking this law was up to five shillings for anyone over fourteen, although there were some exceptions. It took the recent Sunday Trading Act 1994 to permit shops to open on the Sabbath.

Holidays

The introduction of the Holidays With Pay Act 1938 ensured everyone in Britain (not Northern Ireland) was entitled to an annual week's paid holiday. Until this, the poor couldn't afford a holiday as they weren't paid for time off. Scrooge resented Bob Cratchit taking Christmas Day off in *A Christmas Carol*, (1843) although Mr Fezziwig had a more generous attitude. My father remembers when, if

Christmas Day and Boxing Day landed on a weekend, it was hard luck; there were no compensatory days as there are now.

The Bank Holidays Act 1871 declared four bank holidays in England, Wales and Ireland (Easter Monday, Whit Monday, the first Monday in August, and Boxing Day) and five in Scotland (adding New Year's Day); employers were to pay their workers for these days. Christmas Day and Good Friday were automatically included, as were Sundays. Even before this Act, some companies were enlightened. In 1865, Bass, the Burton on Trent brewer, sent 10,000 workers and their families to the seaside on train convoys.

Quaker-owned companies such as chocolate manufacturers Cadbury and Rowntree were among the earliest to give their employees paid time off. As well as introducing the five and a half day week and paid holidays, Cadbury built workers' housing at Bourneville where, by 1900, there were over 300 houses and sports fields. Quaker companies were not exclusive in setting up housing

Taylor's Cricket Team, Newport Pagnell, early 1900s. The Taylors were a noted mustard and soda water manufacturer in the town. Note the straw hats and caps. Social life was important. (Author's collection, ©Adèle Emm)

for workers. Port Sunlight in the Wirral, developed between 1888 and 1914, was built by the Congregationalist soap company Lever Brothers, and there are many other 'model towns'. For a detailed description of the living facilities and chocolate manufacturing process in Bourneville in 1903, see Chapter 4 of *The Food of the Gods* by Brandon Head, **www.gutenberg.org/ebooks/16035** published by Project Gutenberg on the internet.

Many firms had their own brass bands (especially in the north of England), and football and cricket teams to instil a spirit of community in their staff outside their working hours.

Pensions

The first old-age pension as we know it arrived with the Old Age Pension Act 1908, when anyone over seventy in receipt of an annual income less than £31 and ten shillings a year received up to five shillings a week on a sliding scale. Until then, people might work until they dropped, with people describing themselves in census records as shoemakers, general dealers and hat makers well into their seventies. The alternative was Poor Law relief, pauperism and the workhouse – a miserable and bleak old age.

Certain occupations did receive pensions; the army from 1686 and the navy from 1693. The National Archives publish online research guides. A police officer (the London Metropolitan Police was founded in 1829, other police forces a decade later) received a pension after twenty-five years' service. Plenty of genealogical books give advice on researching these.

Workers saved for their old age from their earnings; retirement was never a prospect for many. Quaker Joseph Rowntree (1836– 1925) of York was one of the first to set up a pension scheme for his employees. Terry's' and Rowntrees' archives are at the Borthwick Institute **www.york.ac.uk/borthwick** at York University. The Rowntree archive is online through Discovery (Formerly A2A) **http://discovery.nationalarchives.gov.uk**, but Terry's have no surviving pensions material.

Health and Safety

Generally, until the welfare state and sick leave legislation, an ill worker earned nothing. Health and safety was not as we know it; in fact, it is safe to say there was *no* health and safety. You took your life, literally, in your own hands. Men working in the building trade fell from heights and smiths and butchers lost fingers. In September 1776, nine-year-old thatcher's son William Marsters fell off Guilden Morden church roof. Whether he was a naughty lad climbing there or whether he was working (this was before the 1843 Act) we will never know. What we do know is that the vicar was so shocked by the accident that he recorded how the boy died in the parish register.

Guilden Morden Church, Cambridgeshire. In 1776, nine-year-old thatcher's son William Marsters fell to his death from the roof. (©Adèle Emm)

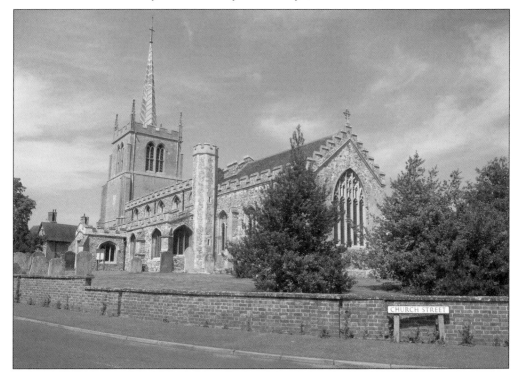

It wasn't just accidents that affected the work force, but also what we now term industrial disease. Lewis Carroll's 'Mad Hatter' was not a whimsical character. Being mad was accepted as a hazard of the hat trade; mercury used in hat making was poisonous (see Chapter 9). Not only was a baker afflicted with dermatitis and 'baker's lung', a form of asthma induced by fine flour, but he was also prone to 'knop knee', an inward-bending knee from carrying an overheavy bread basket on the right arm. Girls working in match-making factories were affected by 'phossie jaw', caused by phosphorus used in the manufacture of matches, which ate away at their teeth and jaws.

Trade Unions and Friendly Societies

In many ways, trade unions fulfil the same function as the former guild system, upholding the rights of members and fighting for better pay and working conditions.

Trade unions stem from the early 1800s when the Industrial Revolution sparked trade disputes. Under the Combination Acts passed in 1799 and 1800 any worker belonging to a trade union could be jailed for up to three months or receive two months' hard labour, but this didn't stop the fight for better pay and working conditions. After the Luddite rebellions of 1811–12 the laws were repealed in 1824 and 1825.

There are many famous incidents of labour unrest besides the 1843 Tolpuddle Martyrs; the Bryant and May match-girl strike in 1888 (the girls are named online), the Great Dock Strike of 1889 and the six-day General Strike of 1926.

A useful source of information on the trade union and Chartist movement is **www.unionancestors.co.uk**, run by Mark Crail, author of *Tracing your Labour Movement Ancestors* (Pen and Sword, 2009). The website lists all trade unions which have existed over the past 200 years, detailing which unions amalgamated to form, for instance, UCATT. Crail runs **www.chartists.net** recording activist ancestors in the 1840s with links to books on Chartism, a useful book for tracing trade union ancestors.

Another useful source for UK trade union members, trade associations and employers is the Modern Record Centre **www2.warwick.ac.uk/services/library/mrc** at Warwick University. Several trade union archives are held here, including those relevant to this book; blacksmiths, forge and smithy, bricklayers, carpenters, iron founders, joiners, painters and stonemasons. The Working Class Movement Library in Salford at **www.wcml.org.uk** is useful for pamphlets, trade union records, personal papers and journals. Genealogical information is on their website at **www.wcml. org.uk/contents/family-history**.

Many workers belonged to friendship societies such as The Ancient Order of Foresters, established 1834 **www.foresters friendlysociety.co.uk**, and The Oddfellows **www.oddfellows. co.uk**, whose Manchester Unity dates back to 1810 with rules from 1730. Originally initiated by people unable to afford the medieval guild livery, rival 'Yeoman Guilds' met in inns, hence why so many pubs are called Oddfellow. In 1832, there were 31,000 members of the Oddfellows, rising to 220,000 by 1842 and 1,028,155 in its 1912 heyday. For a weekly subscription, a member and his family received financial benefits in times of need such as illness, unemployment and death. Oddfellows' records are online (subscription) and include minute books for different towns, membership slips and magazines.

The substantial Foresters' Records are held at the time of writing in Southampton, with plans to move them to Tunstall near Stoke on Trent in the future and **www.aoforestersheritage.com** highlights what is available. A useful resource is *The Federation of Family History Societies An Introduction to Friendly Society Records* by Dr Roger Loman, 2000, now out of print. If your family hailed from Oxfordshire, Shaun Morley's *Oxfordshire Friendly Societies, 1750–1918*, explains vital details and historical notes of 755 societies and branches including crime, courts and brass bands. Some other areas are covered in other publications.

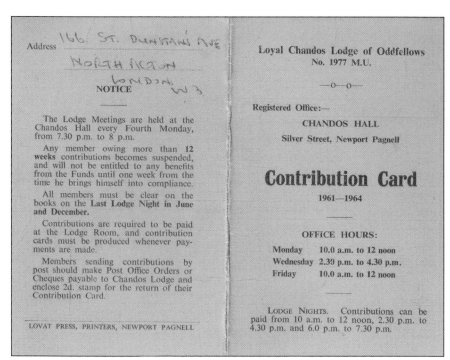

NOTICE

The Lodge Meetings are held at the Chandos Hall every Fourth Monday, from 7.30 p.m. to 8 p.m.

Any member owing more than **12 weeks** contributions becomes suspended, and will not be entitled to any benefits from the Funds until one week from the time he brings himself into compliance.

All members must be clear on the books on the **Last Lodge Night in June and December.**

Contributions are required to be paid at the Lodge Room, and contribution cards must be produced whenever payments are made.

Members sending contributions by post should make Post Office Orders or Cheques payable to Chandos Lodge and enclose 2d. stamp for the return of their Contribution Card.

LOVAT PRESS, PRINTERS, NEWPORT PAGNELL

Loyal Chandos Lodge of Oddfellows
No. 1977 M.U.

—o—o—

Registered Office:—

CHANDOS HALL

Silver Street, Newport Pagnell

Contribution Card

1961—1964

OFFICE HOURS:

Monday 10.0 a.m. to 12 noon
Wednesday 2.30 p.m. to 4.30 p.m.
Friday 10.0 a.m. to 12 noon

LODGE NIGHTS. Contributions can be paid from 10 a.m. to 12 noon, 2.30 p.m. to 4.30 p.m. and 6.0 p.m. to 7.30 p.m.

Oddfellows Contribution Card showing subscriptions. (Author's collection ©Adèle Emm)

No. 401.

Name: Emms W.E.

Contributions per month 5d.

Benefit 18/- per week

Arrears 1961	Cont.	Sig.	Arrears 1962	Cont.	Sig.	Arrears 1963	Cont.	Sig.	Arrears 1964	Cont.	Sig.
Jan. 23			Jan. 22			Jan. 21			Jan. 20		
Feb. 20			Feb. 19			Feb. 18			Feb. 17		
March 20			March 19			March 18	5/5d		March 16	5/5.	BB
April 17			April 16			April 15			April 13		
May 15			May 14			May 13			May 11		
*June 12			*June 11			*June 10			*June 8		
July 10			July 9			July 8			July 6		
August 7			August 6			August 5			August 3		
Sept. 4			Sept. 3			Sept. 2			August 31		
Oct. 2			Oct. 1			Sept. 30			Sept. 28		
Oct. 30	5/5d		Oct. 29			Oct. 28			Oct. 26		
Nov. 27			Nov. 26	5/5d		Nov. 25			Nov. 23		
*Dec. 25			*Dec. 24			*Dec. 23			*Dec. 21		

* Clearing Nights

Chapter 4
MERCHANTS AND MERCERS

The Merchant, to secure his treasure,
Conveys it in a borrowed name.
Matthew Prior (1664-1721)

A merchant was a wholesale dealer exporting and importing from around the world. The most famous, Richard Whittington (1354–1423), Sheriff of London and four times Lord Mayor of London, was not the poor boy so beloved in pantomime, but a younger son despatched from Gloucestershire to London to learn the mercer's trade, making his fortune trading velvet, silk, damask and coal. His cat was not a feline but the colloquial term for collier, the ship transporting coal. Under the terms of his will, this 'rich and pious merchant', founder of a hospital for unmarried mothers, established London's Guildhall Library. A Dick Whittington pub stood near Smithfield Market and Whittington Hospital still treats patients in Archway. What a legacy.

Initially, a mercer was a merchant importing silk, linen and fustian (heavy woven woollen cloth) deemed so important that the Worshipful Company of Mercers heads the Great Twelve Livery Companies. Like similar companies, the Mercers were actively involved in education, founding St Paul's School in 1509.

It was mercer Sir Thomas Gresham (see Chapter 1) who founded the London Stock Exchange in 1565, where merchants met in the main trading hall. Each trade congregated in a different area; West Indian merchants sold rum in one place, with merchants from Turkey trading in another. Foreign merchant met Englishman and business was conducted on a handshake; an Englishman's word was his bond.

Mercer's Maiden on London's Royal Exchange. The symbol of the Company of Mercers is inscribed on all buildings owned by the Company. (©Adèle Emm)

First appearing on a seal in 1425, their heraldic emblem is the Mercer's Maiden, and to this day London buildings owned by the Mercers' Company sport her sign, although some maidens are newly installed. A map of their whereabouts can be found on **www.mercers.co.uk/mercers-maiden-london**.

Over the years, the term mercer came to mean anyone who imported or traded in goods *made* of material, as well as material itself, so a merchant could be either a wholesaler selling to smaller shops or a mere shopkeeper (see Chapter 5).

Of course, London was not the only mercantile port. Bristol, Liverpool and Southampton were other major centres; Bristol and Liverpool were associated with the less appealing aspect of the merchant trade – slavery. The slave triangle saw goods such as guns and brandy taken to Africa and exchanged for slaves sold for rum and sugar in the West Indies and North America and brought back to England.

An interesting if eccentric website by Dan Byrnes in Australia and Ken Cozens in London can be found at **www.merchantnetworks. com.au**. The website includes, among other miscellanea: timelines, names of seventeenth century merchants, a convict contractor list to Australia and an extensive bibliography.

Bristol was important from the sixteenth century with its Society of Merchant Venturers established in 1552, whose members were mostly also members of Bristol Corporation. For background information, see **www.portcities.org.uk**, also covering Hartlepool, Southampton, Bristol, Liverpool and London. For ancestors trading from such seaports, you must search record offices and biographical records are sparse.

Ships and Shipping Resources

Merchants buy and sell. Because so much merchandise originated from abroad, tea, coffee, tobacco and snuff for instance, merchants needed access to a ship and many of them, certainly before 1818 (*Book of Trades*), owned their own. A man's fortune was lost and won through the vagaries of the ocean; a ship lost at sea heralded ruin, a ship arriving in harbour untold wealth. In 1500, London was not among the ten largest cities in the world (*Oxford Encyclopaedia of Economic History*, ed. Joel Mokyr), but by 1814 it was the world's largest port and the gateway to Britain's developing empire, with huge numbers relying on it for their livelihood.

By 1833, the transatlantic crossing generally took twenty-two days. Five years later, steamship *The Great Western* sailed from Bristol to New York taking just fourteen days and twelve hours to complete the passage. In 1840, *The Britannia* crossed the Atlantic in eleven days and four hours. Ships sailing to Australia routinely took seventeen weeks to get there; a seven-month round trip. Compare this to the early navigators who spent months, if not years, at sea. The current transatlantic record is three days, ten hours and forty minutes (1952) by American ocean liner *United States*. Sailing east, before the Suez Canal opened in 1869, ships navigated the notorious Cape of Good Hope at the tip of South Africa. The Panama Canal opened in 1914.

The LMA has plenty of information about shipping, tonnage and taxes financed by London docks. For background information on shipping lines around the world, largely from the nineteenth century but including a few earlier companies including merchants, the World Ship Society at **http://worldshipsociety.org** has books on, for example, the St George Steam Packet Line 1821–43 and East India Company ships (CD only), among others. Based in Chatham, their archives are not open to the public; they have minimal information on individual voyages and nothing on ship personnel.

The East India Company became one of the most powerful companies in the world, even operating its own army. Set up in 1600 by a small group of London merchants, its Royal Charter was bestowed by Queen Elizabeth I. Ships acquired exotic fabrics from abroad and either brought them back to England or took them further east, trading with spices to import into Britain with the fabrics. Dissolved in 1858, its records are held at the British Library in the India Office archives. The index to the records can be searched online via the British Library website at **www.bl.uk**. The pages specific to the East India Office and family history are found on **www.bl.uk/catalogues/iofhs.shtml**.

FindMyPast has baptisms, marriages, burials, wills, pensions, military and civil career information and the India Office Family History Search has biographical information about the British and Europeans in India between 1600 and 1947. Remember, most were not involved specifically in trade and craft, although there is some information about the merchants. For merchants living prior to census records, the first stop is the record office. Another line of enquiry is trade directories, such as *Pigot's*, the Post Office and *Kelly's*.

For anyone with an ancestor who was a citizen and mercer in the City of London, **www.londonroll.org** is a searchable database with information about apprentices for 1339–1900. Names, dates and master's name are given.

Coal Merchants

A practical but now outdated pavement feature in Georgian and Victorian towns and cities such as Bristol, Brighton, Dublin and London (especially Bloomsbury) is the presence of circular metal

Hayward's coalhole cover in Harley Street, London. Their covers can be found all over London and many provincial cities. Hayward's specialised in covers with glass infill. (©Adèle Emm)

plates accessing the cellar. These ensured coal was poured directly into the basement rather than disturbing the residents – in this case, the servants. Unfortunately, coal-holes are rapidly disappearing as pavements are replaced and the function is becoming obsolete. Amongst the most prolific coal-hole cover manufacturers were Hayward Brothers, whose covers occur across cities, especially Bristol and London. Originally glaziers and glass cutters, they bought the business of ironmonger and coal-hole manufacturer Robert Henley in 1848, eventually building their own foundry. An innovative feature of their coal-hole was glass panels inserted into the cover to make the cellar slightly less gloomy. Their history 1783–1953 can be found in *Years of Reflection* on **http://glassian.org/Prism/Hayward/YOR/dj.html**. This chronicle includes their coat of arms and family tree, together with a fascinating history of how events such as the Boer War affected their business.

My mother installed central heating in our house in the 1960s. It ran on coal and we were one of the first people we knew to have it. The coalman regularly delivered cwt (hundredweight – 112lb/eight stone or 50.8kg) sacks from an open-top lorry to our coal shed in the garden. Of course, before central heating everyone had an open fire for heating, cooking or both, and the coalman was a regular visitor to houses everywhere.

Until 1963, coal was sold by the chaldron, a measurement by volume not weight (vulnerable to chicanery), and the chaldron size differed throughout the country. Estimates for the weight of a chaldron depended on location and date and varied from 2,000lb (704kg) in 1421 to 5,940lb (2,690kg) by 1694. A chaldron was the legal limit for a coal cart; too much weight was deemed to damage the road – no one was concerned with horse welfare in those days. A cart carried a maximum of two tons and, because of this weight restriction, a coalman served a relatively small area.

From at least Elizabethan times, collieries were privately owned by landed gentry with coal on their estates. By the seventeenth century, they tended to lease out their collieries, although three Cumbrian families, the Curwens of Workington, the Fletchers of

Distington and the Lowthers of Whitehaven continued to work their own minerals.

Coal tax was levied from at least the reign of James I (1603–25). During the Great Plague of 1665, the price of coal was fixed by the government at 'no more than thirty shillings'. Owners claimed to be operating at a loss and closed their mines. That winter, a ferociously cold one, demand for fuel soared and, with the added crisis of the Great Fire of 1666, the price rocketed to £6 a chaldron. By 1704, to pay for the rebuilding of London, the coal tax had risen from one shilling to seven shillings a chaldron. In 1831, thirteen pence per ton was charged before coal was unloaded from the boat. Coal duties were abolished in 1889–90 and many clerical staff at the Coal Exchange made redundant.

Because the government fixed the price and distribution of coal during the late 1600s as part of the tax system, there was no viable opportunity for coal merchants to trade until the 1800s, although Charringtons **www.coalproducts.co.uk** were in business from 1731. The Cory family, associated with the formation of the Woodmongers' Company circa 1605, was still going strong in 1849.

Effectively, coal merchants were a result of the Industrial Revolution. Factories needed power, the population exploded and there was a huge rise in demand for heat and energy. Until the late seventeenth century, domestic fires were fed by wood or peat for cooking and heating, although how much heating a hovel had is debatable. Burning at a higher temperature, coal was a revolutionary improvement: in 1831 there were 5,167 recorded coal merchants; in 1851 this had risen to 12,092 and by 1871 it was 16,250. Many coal merchants had other occupations as well; one ancestor of mine mended roads, ran a pub and sold coal. Ironmongers commonly sold coal in their shops.

By 1802, a cast-iron range could be found in well-heeled urban kitchens. By 1848, the main source of fuel for London was coal and a household might burn a ton a month. To supply the fireplaces of London nearly 3.5 million tons of coal was transported each year by ship (called sea coal) from the coalfields of Northumberland and

Durham to Billingsgate Docks of fish fame. Men lived for weeks on board ships between Newcastle and London. It took 12,000 shiploads and 3,000 vessels to transport it and the subsequent coal tax revenue funded building works such as the Thames Embankment.

After the 1850s, coal arrived mainly by train. In 1875, eight million tons of coal was transported to London, five million by train and three by sea. No wonder London was plagued by pea-soupers! On arrival, coal was unloaded, graded and sold, the market price set according to how much coal was available that day. Sales were conducted privately between sellers and buyers.

Coal factors were middle-men buying coal from collieries and taking it by cart (later lorry) to be distributed to coal merchants, although some collieries employed factors directly; these were paid commission to sell coal to merchants. Factors in the London Coal Exchange were intermediary agents between sellers and purchasers and again received a percentage of the deal as commission, although it was possible to sell one's own coal without using a factor. The Coal Factors' Society was established in the first half of the eighteenth century for people engaged in the wholesale coal trade in London. By 1832, it had become a 'mutual protection' society. Dating from 1761, its archives, consisting largely of an alphabetical list of ships, their tonnage, minutes, attendance books, financial records, lists of prices of coal and contracts with people for the supply of barges and so on, are held in the LMA.

From 1770, London coal merchants acquired their coal from the London Coal Exchange, opened to regulate the trade on the north side of Thames Street, almost opposite Billingsgate Market. It suffered considerable damage in the Blitz. After the Second World War, the coal industry was nationalised.

Coal bought from the London docks or the railway station was bagged by hand, put on a cart and transported to customers. For those outside London, coal was sourced direct from the mines (e.g. Cheshire, Derbyshire, Kent, Lancashire, Scotland, Wales and Yorkshire) or collected from the station. Water transport was an option via navigable rivers and canals where coal merchants collected from hubs. Blacksmiths (see Chapter 7) generally sourced their coke from the nearest gas works, where an enterprising coal merchant also acquired coke, cheaper than coal, for his poorer customers.

Before the First World War, most coal merchants' yards were wooden sheds near railway sidings which were, of course, their coal source. A coalman's yard needed space to stable horses and store coal and cart. Outgoings included horse-feed, the farrier and occasional trips to the wheelwright. The exit roads from the sidings sloped and coal carts were fitted with skid pans under the rear wheels. When these failed, as they commonly did, horse and runaway load frequently crashed into houses, shops and gardens.

During the inter-war suburb expansion building boom, railway companies built small coal offices near stations on the high street; far more convenient for coalman and customer. They can still be spotted, although the business will have changed.

It was possible to make large amounts of money from selling coal. Cesar Picton (c.1755–1836), a black African slave brought to England in 1761, used a £100 legacy to set up as a coal merchant. He bought a house in Thames Ditton, Surrey, in 1816 for £4,000! Conversely, Samuel Plimsoll (1824–1898) became a London coal merchant in 1854 only to be left destitute when his business failed. When his fortunes changed, he became MP for Derby, successfully campaigning for the introduction of the Plimsoll line on ships. During the last decade of the nineteenth century, coal merchants' businesses struggled because of coal workers' industrial action.

The first reference to the Worshipful Company of Fuellers **www.fuellers.co.uk** (originally the Company of Woodmongers and Coal Sellers) is in 1376, but they weren't awarded their first Royal Charter until 1605. Their main responsibility was to collect coal tax. The Company surrendered its charter after the Great Fire of London and other bodies represented the coal industry. It was re-formed in 1981 to cater for the energy industry. R.S. Brown's *Digging for History in the Coal Merchants' Archives*, 1988, mentions a large amount of archives including society minute books from 1842 (earlier minutes have been lost) and scrap books containing letters, handbills, booklets and prints from the 1820s. It is unlikely that they hold archives of relevance to the family historian.

The Coal Trade Benevolent Association, founded in 1888 by the Colliery Agents and Coal Salesmen's Association, first met in the Coal Exchange to 'dispense charitable relief' to people who had worked in the coal-selling industry. Unfortunately, no beneficiary archives are held by either the Benevolent Association or the Coal Merchants' Federation.

For those searching for information about coal merchant ancestors, there is little available. Rootsweb, family history websites and forums are full of posts about former coal merchants and their businesses with greater and lesser success. If your family ran an established firm, you may get more response than for a one-man operation. As is usual with local firms and businesses, more satisfaction may be gained at the local family history centre and library, where photographs and archives relating to coal merchant ancestors might be available. Don't be too disappointed if there is nothing on a one-man-band operation. Records offices may help; for instance, Cambridge holds land purchases for several coal merchants and they have coal merchants Coote and Warren's Wisbech depot's cash book 1907–09.

The British Newspaper Archive (subscription) and physically searching local newspapers may produce results, but this is unlikely to be quick. You may find information in the Discovery archives **http://discovery.nationalarchives.gov.uk**: for instance, in 1841 William Emms stole coal from Thomas Gibbs, a Stratford upon Avon coal merchant. Also try **www.aim25.ac.uk/cgi-bin/vcdf/search?key word=Coal%20merchants&acc_type=1&nv1=browse&nv2=sub**.

Coffee, Chocolate, Tea Merchants; Shops and Houses

We think of Britain as a nation of tea drinkers but when they were first imported, coffee and chocolate were the beverages of choice – none with today's respectable reputation.

In 1651, Alexander Hay bought a brew-house in the Pool of London and from 1710 the eponymous Hay's Wharf was the most important for unloading tea, coffee and cocoa. This part of the Pool of London became 'London's Larder', with foodstuffs, potatoes, hops, cider and lamb imported and stored here – it has now been converted to apartments and offices. Tea, coffee and chocolate were imported by merchants and dealers and sold on.

The East India Company placed its first order for 100lb of China tea in 1664. By 1685, this figure had increased to 12,070lb, swamping the market as tea was less popular than coffee, gin and ale. Once tea arrived in England, it was sold at auction and bought in bulk to sell generally to dealers around the country who sold to smaller dealers and teashops. At this time, the only *legal* tea importer was the East India Company.

Walpole (1676–1745) introduced taxes on tea, chocolate and coffee in 1724, which affected the East India Company more than the consumer. The only way most people could afford it was to buy illegally imported tea smuggled alongside tobacco and brandy in such quantities that the East India Company lost huge amounts of money. By 1750, the East India Company was importing over four and a half million pounds of tea, charging what it liked because of its monopoly. In the 1770s, London tea merchant Richard Eagleton, selling his tea from the Grasshopper Tea Warehouse in Bishopsgate Street, advertised tea at four to fifteen shillings per pound, which, when a tradesman earned ten shillings a week, equates to more than an average man's weekly salary. Nor is it surprising that, to boost sales, for every quarter pound of tea sold, Eagleton entered his customers into a prize-winning lottery.

In 1706, Thomas Twining bought a coffee shop in The Strand, London, proceeding to sell tea in the neighbouring shop. It was a risky enterprise. When he set up business, the price of legally imported tea was an exorbitant fourteen to thirty shillings a pound. In 1784, his grandson Richard Twining successfully lobbied the government to reduce the tax in the Commutation Act. Although tea was still imported by the East India Company, smuggling ceased

Twinings tea merchant's doorway, The Strand, London. Established in 1706, Twinings is the longest surviving business on the same premises in London without changing name or commodity. (©Adèle Emm)

virtually overnight. The Twining shop and museum claims the record for the longest surviving business on the same London premises without changing name, ownership or commodity. For anyone with a Twining in their ancestry, the shop and museum posts its family tree on the walls, plus a history of tea importation into this country.

In 1813, the East India Company lost its trade monopoly with India with many questioning its continued monopoly of the China tea trade, still the major source of tea. In 1834, a Tea Committee investigated the possibility of growing tea in India and by 1888 Indian tea imports exceeded those from China.

1870 to 1878 were regarded as the 'China tea years', with the *Cutty Sark*, perhaps the most famous tea clipper (although not the fastest), departing from London in February 1870 with beer, wine and spirits. It returned from Shanghai nearly ten months later with around 1,450 tons of tea. This was a fast trip; imagine how much longer it took for tea merchants in the 1700s.

Chronologically, the taste for coffee arrived first. England's first coffeehouse opened in Oxford in 1652 where, for a penny, you could enter the premises and drink a cup of coffee. Alcohol wasn't served and the tenor of the coffeehouse was witty and intelligent conversation, gaining the epithet of 'penny university', because for the entrance fee you received an education. Women were generally (not everywhere) banned. The second oldest coffeehouse, also in Oxford, The Queen's Lane Coffee House established in 1654, is, at the time of writing, still trading. London's first coffee shop opened in Cornhill in 1652 when coffee importer Daniel Edwards helped his former servant Pasqua Rosee set it up.

There were rules; no swearing or fighting and transgressors were fined a shilling or had to buy a cup of coffee. Gambling, dice and cards were forbidden. Becoming centres of political debate (Pepys enjoyed the coffeehouse), their popularity increased so that by 1675, there were more than 3,000 coffeehouses in England. By 1739, some of the 551 coffeehouses in London were influential business centres – the insurance company Lloyds of London was named after Edward Lloyd's coffeehouse in Tower Street where it started in 1688. Coffeehouses were a short-lived fad; by the late eighteenth century, they had all but disappeared.

Cocoa beans arrived in England in the late seventeenth century although Europe had imported them from the end of the sixteenth century. Like tea and coffee, it was an expensive import which only the wealthy could afford. The first chocolate house opened in Gracechurch Street, London, in 1657 – a mere five years after the coffeehouse. Also served in coffee shops, its higher price warranted less of a following apart from exclusive clubs such as White's of St James's – still exclusive, and the only female visitor has been Queen Elizabeth II. Some elite chocolate houses were politically influential – the Cocoa Tree in Pall Mall was the informal headquarters of the Tory Party – but most were regarded as hotbeds of insurrection. Chocolate house Ozindas, also in St James's, was raided in 1715 for Jacobite conspirators. As chocolate was marketed as an aphrodisiac, by the 1730s many chocolate houses were scenes of debauchery, reflecting the reputation of the teahouse. William Hogarth (1697–1764) satirised White's as a form of hell in *Rake's Progress* (1733).

George I (1660–1727) was an enthusiastic devotee of hot chocolate. He was served his morning cuppa by Thomas Tosier, who prepared the beverage using a charcoal stove and a spit for roasting the cocoa beans. Tosier's wife, Grace, ran a chocolate house in Greenwich. Their recipe for drinking chocolate is unlike today's. Stored as patties like large chocolate buttons, it was often mixed with alcohol and served thick and rich with sugar and spices such as cardamom, cinnamon and black pepper.

Right from their inception in the mid-seventeenth century, teahouses had a racy, raucous, scandalous reputation to be avoided at all costs by respectable women who drank tea as a social event at home. For high society ladies, afternoon tea filled the long gap between luncheon at one and dinner at seven, achieving acceptance with the middle classes from the 1860s. As for the teashop as we know it, the temperance movement influenced their rise in the high street from the 1880s and it was only from then on that they were patronised by 'decent' women.

From 1660 to 1689, teashop tea tasted considerably different to today's because tax was charged in *liquid* form. Tea was brewed in the morning, inspected by the excise officer who extorted the levy, stored in barrels and reheated as required. Stewed indeed! From 1689, tax was levied on *leaf*, not liquid, so it isn't surprising that Twining launched his successful teashop when it tasted better. Sugar, another expensive import, was added to tea in the seventeenth century. Milk was deemed unusual, although there is a veritable internet debate on the subject. For the middle-class Georgian, it was the rise in the price of ale and alcohol (due to the higher price of malt), together with the abolition of import tax, that made tea and coffee increasingly affordable and eventually the staple drink, much as it is today.

Apart from the male preserve of tea and coffee shops in London, you are unlikely to find an ancestor running a beverage shop before the 1870s; they are more likely to be tea merchants and grocers and any information prior to the census, such as it is, is found in directories e.g. Post Office, *Pigot's* and *Kelly's*. Catherall and Butcher, tea dealers, are listed in the 1819 London post office directory at 92 Pall Mall. It was common for tradesmen to 'mix and match' their products; William Emms of Syleham Mill, Norfolk, (1834–1908) was both a tea dealer and draper. As usual, a trip to the record office may be profitable, but there may be little specific information. It is enough to know that, until the mid to late Victorian age, tea, coffee and chocolate shops were unsavoury places where respectable women feared to tread…

Mercers

Unlike the original meaning of the word, if a man in a suburban high street described himself as a mercer in the census, he was probably a general dealer selling all and sundry in a shop. James Hambleton, whose carved stone shop sign can still be seen above a house in Alstonefield, Staffordshire, is one such example, styling himself 'Mercer and Grocer – Dealer in coffee, tea, tobacco and snuff'.

His family and business can be easily traced through the census records. A veritable powerhouse of ambition, not only was he a dealer, but he also farmed fifty-two acres, and rising, as well as being a shopkeeper (1861) with live-in apprentices. In 1881, when the shop was also the post office, his brother helped out as shop assistant. In 1841, his son described himself as a grocer. Effectively, if an ancestor describes himself as mercer in a census, especially in a small town or village, regard him as a shopkeeper and turn to Chapter 5.

London Mercers' records 1339–1900 can be checked via **www.londonroll.org**. Lisa Jefferson's *Medieval Accounts Books of the Mercers of London edited and translated* might be of use.

Tobacconists and Tobacco Merchants

In his 1936 short story *The Verger* Somerset Maugham (1874–1965) tells of a church verger who, losing his job through illiteracy and desperate for a cigarette to console himself, establishes a tobacconist's and makes his fortune. Every high street had one, dedicated to selling cigars, cigarettes, rolling tobacco, tobacco and cigarette boxes, snuff, pipes, matches, lighters and other paraphernalia. Many blended their own tobacco. Standing sentinel outside, especially those selling cigars, was a large wooden statue of a native American known as a 'Virginian' in the trade. They can still, increasingly rarely, be found and, at the time of writing, there was one outside a shop in Windsor Station.

Tobacco was discovered in the 'New World' at the end of the sixteenth century. Sir Francis Drake introduced pipe smoking in 1572 and by 1585 had persuaded Sir Walter Raleigh to take it up. By 1614 there were reputedly over 7,000 'tobagies' in and around London selling tobacco. Pipes were sold in apothecaries, grocers, alehouses and general dealers. As tobacco was regularly adulterated with oil, spices and aniseed to make it heavier, sellers had a poor reputation and there were attempts to license the trade in 1633 when those deemed worthy to retail it were certified by their local Justices of the Peace. After February 1634, retailing tobacco was forbidden without a licence (Royal Proclamations of Charles I 1625–46) and licences were granted by letters patent with summaries in the Calendars of State Papers, Domestic from 1634 onwards. These are available in the National Archives, Kew.

By 1620, the cultivation of tobacco was banned in England; Virginia in America was given the monopoly to grow it and trade with England. Almost immediately, tobacco was subject to taxation. In 1604, James I, a notable opponent of smoking, increased the import tax exponentially. By 1620 it was a whopping shilling a pound, although down to nine pence a pound a year later. Closely associated with the slave trade, tobacco was imported alongside tea and coffee and was equally one of the most smuggled commodities.

As soon as tobacco arrived from the New World, clay pipes were manufactured to consume it. From 1580, Newington was London's main manufacturing area, but Brosely in Shropshire (from 1575), Bristol (from 1616), Peterborough, Portsmouth and Newcastle upon Tyne were other important centres. There are many archaeological studies on clay pipe manufacture and, as pipes were personalised with the maker's mark, you might discover an ancestor's specific pipe mark. A website for London pipe makers is **http://archive.museumoflondon.org.uk/claypipes**. Outside London, including European pipe makers, try the Society for Clay Pipe research at **http://scpr.co/Links.html** or the National Pipe Archive at **www.pipearchive.co.uk/links.html**. From the nineteenth century, Briarwood and Meerschaums replaced clay pipes.

The Worshipful Pipe Makers and Tobacco Blenders Company **www.tobaccolivery.co.uk** (charter 1619) restricted manufacture of clay pipes to London, seriously harming trade elsewhere, especially Bristol, until the restrictions were removed in 1639. In 1660 the 'Exportation of Wooll Woolfells Fullers Earth or any kinde of Scouring Earth' (i.e. clay suitable for making clay pipes) was prohibited to protect the English cloth industry, as clay was a substitute for fuller's earth. In 1695, there was an attempt to tax tobacco pipes but, deemed a failure, it was repealed in 1699.

After Charles II returned from exile in Paris in 1660, snuff was popularised, especially among English aristocrats, and for a century or two was considered an upper-class habit.

In 1614, Seville in Spain was the centre of cigar making, with cigars arriving in Britain circa 1815 after the Napoleonic wars with France. Matches were invented in 1852. Cigarettes, literally 'small cigars', were introduced in France from the 1830s, becoming popular in England from the 1840s when Philip Morris opened his shop in

Bond Street selling expensive hand-rolled Turkish cigarettes. It took the Crimean War, during which British soldiers watched Russians and Turks rolling their own, for cigarettes to achieve mass appeal. Robert Gloag, a Crimean war veteran, opened the first cigarette factory in England in 1856. They were expensive; a skilled cigarette maker made four a minute. This rose to 200 a minute when American James Albert Bonsack (1859–1924) won an 1875 challenge by Allen & Ginter of Richmond, Virginia, to devise a cigarette rolling machine. The prize was $75,000.

One of the most famous tobacco importers and cigarette manufacturers was Henry Overton Wills (1761–1826) who opened a shop in Castle Street, Bristol, in 1786. His company became W.D. and H.O. Wills, now Imperial Tobacco. The first Wills cigarette, initially hand-rolled in their London factory, was the Bristol (1871). Woodbines arrived in 1888 and Capstan Full Strength in 1894. From 1887, they were among the first companies including advertising cards – the cigarette card – in their packets. In 1877, Nottingham-based John Player bought William Wright's Broadmarsh tobacco factory, founded in 1832. Player was responsible for the Navy Cut brands and revolutionised rolling tobacco circa 1880 by selling it in tins to keep it fresh. Before this, smokers bought tobacco by weight in ounces, storing it in boxes.

For those seeking information about tobacconist forebears, any information, such as it is, will be in local record offices. Initially, try merchants who imported tea, coffee and sugar. If you are lucky enough to have tobacconists or clay pipe makers from Newcastle or Gateshead up to circa 1800 in your family, you may find them and sources (e.g. parish records and wills) in Lloyd J. Edwards' MA thesis for Durham University, published online at **http://etheses. dur.ac.uk/6882**. Guilds and wills may be helpful. Be warned, some early references to tobacconists relate to tobacco *merchants* and not shopkeepers who, especially from the nineteenth century when there was so much competition, sold other commodities alongside tobacco products.

Victuallers

Originally, a victualler was a purveyor of provisions, especially for the navy, but came to mean a licensed pub owner. Licensed ale house keepers, the victuallers, traded to the hoi polloi; the vintners were wine dealers in the luxury market. There were alehouses before the Romans and, in late 2013, Japanese archaeologists unearthed the tomb of an Egyptian beer brewer in Luxor, dating it at over 3,000 years old.

Alehouses were licensed from the mid-sixteenth century in order, as today, to reduce perceived levels of drunkenness and social disorder. Under the Alehouse Act 1552, anyone selling beer or ale required the consent of the local Justices of the Peace, granted either before the full sessions of the peace or before two justices. The alehouse keeper had to ensure good behaviour or risk paying a fine and/or losing his licence. Records, if they exist, are held in record offices and give name, parish, details of the surety and their tavern sign, which was how, at the time of high illiteracy, people recognised an alehouse.

Between the Licensing Act of 1753 and the Beer Act of 1830, new licences were only granted to people producing certificates of good character signed by parish notables. After the Licensing Act of 1828 until the 1869 Wine and Beerhouse Act, selling beer was a virtual free for all. A beerhouse, incidentally, was exactly that; a room in a house where beer was served, often from a jug. In my family-run beerhouse, beer was served in the front room and the cellar, only three steps down, reached by a door in the hall.

The Beer Act of 1830 dissolved many of the controls and anyone who paid the poor rate could sell beer, ale and cider without a licence by taking out an excise licence from the Excise authorities. Effectively, if your family ran a beerhouse or has 'licensed victualler' on their census records, there may be no licensing information between 1828 and 1872.

In 1872, Gladstone, on a 'drink-is-the-curse-of-the-working-man' crusade, introduced the Intoxicating Liquor (licensing) Act to promote sobriety and encourage hardworking men to save for their retirement. Not only did clerks of the licensing divisions have to keep a register of all licences, but in areas deemed to have too many beerhouses, magistrates could close them down. The Act forced pubs to close at midnight in towns and 11pm in the countryside so agricultural labourers could walk home by midnight. The Act also prohibited the adulteration of beer at a time when salt was added to make people drink more. Modern day peanuts on tables have the same effect…

For a family historian, there are plenty of resources. A newspaper report describes my ancestor's trial for plying a customer with drink when he had had too much; she was acquitted. Licences can be checked at local and county record offices' catalogues, which generally index what they have. Googling the name of the pub or beerhouse, often listed in the census records, brings up a list of licensees and details of court cases. A useful site is **http://pubshistory.com**. Another helpful site is the eponymous **www.closedpubs.co.uk** which relates their fate. The Brewery History Society **www.breweryhistory.com** has a database of breweries and The Pub History Society at **www.pubhistory society.co.uk** has explanations of licencing laws. For anyone with a victualler in Warwickshire, there is an online list from the quarter sessions records of all victuallers in Warwickshire from 1801 to 1828. As the URL is ridiculously long, the easiest way is a Boolean search with 'victuallers' database' and 'Warwickshire County Council'. The information given is: name of the victualler, where they are located, date and any bondsmen. **www.genguide.co.uk/source/publican-brewery-and-licensed-victuallers-records-occupations/127/** gives a bibliography for books on countywide and more localised pubs and brewers. For an excellent guide to Newport Pagnell pubs, see *One More for the Road* by Donald Hurst and Dennis Mynard. Local newspapers add more information but you need a date to avoid scrolling through endless pages.

Family anecdotes add local colour. My family has tales of a poker kept in the fire for plunging into ale; pints of beer paid for by rabbit or large fish (both poached) and barrels floating in the cellar when the river flooded. Details can be double-checked in local newspapers.

Death certificates reveal hazards of the trade. Predictably, beerhouse owners and publicans often died of cirrhosis. Many publicans made a lot of money. A quick glance through the probate records reveals how much. In 1861 William Emm, victualler of the Queen's Arms by Watford Station, left £1,000. However, not everybody made that kind of money.

London's Licensed Victualler's Benevolent Institution founded the Licensed Victuallers' Asylum for retired, ill and distressed licensed victuallers in the Old Kent Road in 1827. An asylum in this sense meant sanctuary – not to be confused with a workhouse or lunatic asylum. Completed by 1843, it consisted of 101 three-roomed one-storey homes, a chapel and library, set around two lawns. Residents received a small weekly allowance, which increased to a maximum of twelve shillings for couples and eight shillings for a single person as well as a supply of coal and access to doctors and medicines. If an inmate had been a member of the Licensed Victualler's Company, they received an extra shilling a week; a considerably more compassionate existence than the workhouse. If your ancestors were here, their names are in the census records. For further information, see **www.british-history.ac.uk/report.aspx? compid=45279** or **http://asylumlondon.org/history**. The Company also established a school in Kennington Lane with new premises in 1837. The school moved to Slough in 1921.

Vintners/Wine Merchants

Vintners traded in luxury goods selling wine to a wealthy clientele and in the Middle Ages, according to the Company of Vintners website **www.vintnershall.co.uk**, nearly one third of England's trade between 1446 and 1448 was wine importation – a huge proportion and vintners in charge! The name is derived from the medieval wine merchants' original meeting place, St Martin the

Vintry. Eleventh in the Great Twelve Livery Companies of London, their charter is dated 1363 when they were granted a monopoly trade deal with Gascony, France; by the sixteenth century their rights were heavily curtailed.

During the early days of the English Civil War in 1643 when Parliament was desperate to fill its coffers, it was discovered that no excise had been paid within ten miles of London. An ordinance was given requiring the Vintners 'to bring in the money due for the half excise of all wines remaining in their hands at or before the eleventh of September last.' I do not know what happened…

The Vintners lost both hall and records in the Great Fire but, although they regained some standing during the reign of William and Mary, they never regained their previous dominance and by 1725 vintners tended not to join the Company. Together with the Crown and the Dyers, the Vintners are the legal owners of all swans on the River Thames (two swans with bunches of grapes around their necks appear on the Vintners' coat of arms) and they continue swan upping to this day. The pub name, the Swan with Two Necks, alternatively Two Nicks, allegedly derives from this practice.

The vintner did not just buy and sell wine. According to Physician Walter Charleton's (1619–1707) discourse *The Vintner's Mystery Display'd, Or, The Whole Art of the Wine Trade Laid Open*, published circa 1700, purporting to expose the tricks of the vintners' trade, in terms of maintaining profit, they needed to store wine for the best conditions and rescue any which had gone sour.

The Vintners' legacy continued into the Victorian era. Like the Victuallers, they set up almshouses/asylums in London from land left to the Company in 1446 by Guy Shuldham. Unfortunately, they too were destroyed by the Great Fire. In 1676, twelve alms houses were erected in Mile End, which were rebuilt in 1801. Destroyed again by the Blitz in 1941, The Vintry, at Nutley, Surrey, was built in the late 1950s. The archives for these almshouses are held in Guildhall Library. If your ancestor was a vintner, apprenticed to one or even worked as a licenced victualler, you may find records of them here or, of course, in the local archives.

Berry Bros & Rudd, founded 1698, trades under the sign of the coffee mill, clearly seen here. (©Adèle Emm)

Berry Bros & Rudd at 3 St James Street, London, was founded in 1698 as a grocer supplying coffee to nearby coffeehouses. Unusually for its time, it was founded by a woman, Widow Bourne, and subsequently run by daughter Elizabeth Pickering under the sign of the coffee mill which still swings outside the premises. Dating from the early eighteenth century, the building is something of a time warp and well worth a visit. As a family firm, there are no records of anyone who worked there. Hatshop Lock & Co. (see Chapter 9) is a neighbour.

Chapter 5
SHOPKEEPERS

England is a nation of Shopkeepers.
Napoleon Bonaparte (1769–1821) quoting Adam Smith

From the eleventh or twelfth century, everyone made their way to their nearest market town by foot, horseback or cart to buy produce they couldn't make or grow themselves. The alternative was to hope a pedlar or chapman walked past the cottage carrying what was needed – or do without. Depending on the royal charter, a market

Windsor Guildhall and Market Street. Covered market places became common from the early 1800s. (©Adèle Emm)

was held one or two days a week and is often held on the same day today. Under the gaze of the market cross, still standing at Salisbury, Malmesbury and Stalbridge among others, this medieval shopping precinct was where sellers, who paid a few pence to the lord of the manor for the privilege, displayed their produce on stalls, baskets or laid out in front of them. Market squares were open to the elements until the late 1700s or early 1800s when, in a spirit of gentrification, the good burghers built town halls, guildhalls and covered areas for the market stalls, many of which can still be seen. Examples include the town hall in Bridport, Godalming's Pepperpot, Bath, Windsor and Stockport's produce hall, built in 1851 and nicknamed the Hen Market.

Medieval 'permanent' shops doubled, like today, as housing; shop at the front, shutters opening onto the street through which the trader passed goods to the customer, and living quarters either at the back or above.

During the rebuilding of London after the Great Fire, small glass windows (George Ravenscroft patented lead crystal glass in 1674) glazed some shops but, because of the cost, took a while to be established. Contemporary drawings of Kensington High Street in 1811 show neat Georgian buildings with shops at street level illuminated by windows made up of small panes – large ones were expensive due to manufacturing costs and the glass tax (withdrawn 1845). London's Burlington Arcade, which opened in 1819, is an example of an early, arguably the first, purpose-built shopping mall. Regent Street, designed by John Nash, was one of the first planned shopping streets in England, with covered colonnades to keep the shopper dry (later demolished), which opened in 1825. After the invention of plate glass in 1848 by the pioneer Chance Brothers of Birmingham alongside Pilkington, large glass windows became more popular. Chance's employee records have been catalogued – see the Black Country website – and are held at Sandwell's Archive Services.

For anyone living in a rural area prior to the early 1800s, a shop was a luxury. Early shops were general dealers, buying and selling anything and everything as and when they acquired it. The owner was responsible for sourcing merchandise, so the better the transport system, the more variety there was. Luxury goods from abroad such as tea, coffee, sugar, rum, tobacco and silk, many imported by the East India Company (see Chapter 4), became available from the late seventeenth century. Highly taxed, they were of course only available at a premium in larger towns and cities. During the Georgian period various products were mass produced for the first time and available in upmarket shops; Staffordshire pottery was a prime example. After the introduction of railways, agents known as travellers journeyed from town to village with samples for shopkeepers to buy and sell to their customers.

The golden age of the individual shop was the early twentieth century when anything and everything could be bought on the local high street, from the butcher, baker, grocer, haberdasher, milliner,

Bedford High Street, c.1907, showing the variety of shops. (Author's collection, ©Adèle Emm)

ironmonger, pharmacy – often several of each, providing healthy competition close to home. The customer patronised their favourite shop with friendly but deferential, often obsequious, service; no need to carry heavy bags for, at a charge, the shop-boy delivered the goods to the customer's home.

The proprietor of a shop was generally male and most businesses were family run with younger members working as shop assistants. Should the man be taken ill or die, it was common for his widow to continue the business. Extra help was hired as required and recorded in census records; evidence that the business was prosperous enough to employ someone from outside the family. Some businesses, milliners and dressmakers for example, were run by women, usually in their own homes. I suspect one of my ancestors disinherited his son for marrying a 'mere' milliner who, as it happened, supported her husband when he was unemployed and ran the business on her own terms after his premature death.

Most shop assistants lived in, which entailed duties around the house as well as in the shop serving, cleaning and displaying the goods. Days off and time for lunch depended on the benevolence of the shop owner. For more money, assistants ran the shop when the proprietor was absent, interviewed travellers and ordered stock.

Shops were open late to catch people coming home from work, theatre or pub. Eventually, the 1904 Shops Act limited those under eighteen to working a shocking seventy-four hour week. In other words, no restrictions for over eighteens and longer hours before the Act! A fifteen-year-old girl recorded arduous twelve-hour days in 1910 for five to six shillings a week.

All changed for everyone under the Shops Act of 1911, which stipulated a maximum sixty-hour working week, half a day off each week – early closing day – and compulsory washing facilities in each shop.

Sunday shopping in the UK is relatively recent (1994), although medieval customers had no such restrictions. However, the Sunday Observance Act of 1781 forced shops to close on Sunday as well as parks, theatres, museums and taverns. Amusement was severely limited, especially for the poor inhibited by lack of light and space at home and, of course, illiteracy.

The department store was a city feature. Although similar emporiums existed from the 1790s (Harding Howell and Co. in Pall Mall, London; Harrods from1834; Kendal Milne and Faulkner founded in Manchester in 1836) the main growth of the department store was from the 1860s onwards. These large stores needed assistants and many were women paid half a man's wage. Men had other options; emigration or factory work paid more. Notwithstanding, these women earned considerably more than a dressmaker or factory worker and had the added benefit, albeit heavily restricted, of living-in, usually in dormitories on the top floor or nearby hostels. It was a skilled job; they had to add up quickly in their heads, package parcels prettily, speak courteously and dress respectably to work in Derry and Toms in Kensington High Street (founded 1862), Whiteley's in Westbourne Grove (1863) and the Co-operative Wholesale Society founded in Rochdale the same year. Selfridges, a relative newcomer, opened its doors in Oxford Street in 1909 where, unlike other department stores, female assistants did not live in.

As described in Emily Faithfull's *Choice of a Business for Girls* of 1864 (see **http://gerald-massey.org.uk/faithfull**), a female shop assistant could earn between £20 and £50 a year including board and lodging with relatively pleasant working conditions if she didn't mind standing for long hours and being tactful with demanding and difficult customers. Working inside in a clean environment was far more pleasant than life on a farm, in a factory or washing and charring. Of course, there were industrial diseases associated with standing for long hours, 'standing evil' as it was known; indigestion, varicose veins, swollen feet, anaemia, headaches and fainting.

Census records in 1871 reveal 120,000 female shop workers. By 1881, there were 140,000 and in 1901 this had risen to over 250,000.

Many department stores have archives. The Co-op's archives are held in Manchester **www.archive.coop** and can be visited by prior appointment Monday to Friday. They also hold archives for their regional societies and the website collections page explains what records are available. County records offices also hold records for the Co-op; for instance Norfolk has apprentice records for 1894–1916 (BR 247/66) for e.g. Lillie Arnold, draper, 1894 and Percy W. Crown, grocer, 1913. John Lewis, which started life in 1864 as a draper in Oxford Street, has two full-time archivists, but the archives, held in Cookham, Berkshire, and open to the public on Saturdays from 10am to 4pm, hold little of genealogical interest. Whiteley's archives are held at the City of Westminster Archive Centre, see **www.nationalarchives.gov.uk** for details. For stores which joined the House of Fraser group, Glasgow University holds the archives and the catalogue is on **www.housefraserarchive.ac.uk**. Click on the home page/companies to see what is available. This excellent website gives details of store founders, shop history and, in some cases, the living conditions and background to department store workers including an online photo collection. Selfridges' archives are held privately.

Originally, the word *monger* was disparaging and derived, it is thought, from *mangere*, a 'dealer in slaves' and *manganeuein* (Greek) 'to use trickery'. It is still used pejoratively in warmonger and scandalmonger. The old English meaning of *monger* meant 'dealer' as in ironmonger, fishmonger, cheesemonger and costermonger.

Shopkeepers were not averse to cheating for profit. Common practice for unscrupulous traders was to sell inferior goods from the back rather than the perfect ones on display, slipping in a rotten apple for instance. Food was often adulterated; white lead was added to flour, ground glass to sugar, red lead to coffee and so on. The Food and Drugs Act of 1860 attempted to keep food uncontaminated – additives became a criminal offence. Initially, and because it wasn't binding, the Act was ineffective due to a lack of obligation by local authorities to pay for chemical analysis to check for adulteration. Perhaps the term *manganeuein* was spot on.

For many trades such as bakers and butchers, a sweep through pre-1841 directories such as the Post Office, *Pigot's* and *Kelly's* (found online at FindMyPast and Ancestry, or as printed directories in family history centres), may reveal the address where an ancestor lived and worked before the 1841 census although, of course, there are no details for the rest of the family. Advertisements in local newspapers, printed on the front page until the early twentieth century depending on the newspaper, give details about contemporary prices and sales. Unfortunately, if your relative worked as a shop assistant for a small local store, there may be little information and you may never discover where they worked. For those tracing back to guilds, record offices are the places to visit with their excellent catalogues, although you must physically go through the records to find any information. Discovery **http://discovery. nationalarchives.gov.uk** may throw up references to your ancestors.

What follows is a general view in alphabetical order of the background to shops and *specific* sources for their trade. As always, record offices are key.

Bakers and Confectioners

One of my ancestors travelled from Oxfordshire to Lancashire as a journeyman baker, hawking bread around Ashton under Lyne from the back of a cart. As a boy in the 1890s, my grandfather, brought up in a baker's household, paid his way by catching and harnessing the carthorse each morning to deliver bread around the villages of Buckinghamshire. In 1851, his grandfather, Caleb Masters, was a journeyman baker in Newport Pagnell living at the Coleman family bakery. By 1861, Caleb Jnr owned his own bakery and confectioners in the High Street, employing a journeyman baker of his own and living and working in the same premises until circa 1900, when his end of the High Street was demolished for the new Co-op. His neighbours, a milliner and cabinet maker, were victims of the same development. Moving around the corner, he set up a general provision shop with his second wife. Once a shop keeper, always a shop keeper.

Caleb Masters' bakery, High Street, Newport Pagnell, awaiting demolition in 1904 for the new Co-op. His shop is flanked by a milliner and cabinet maker. Family legend had it that the photo was taken because of the snow, rare in Newport Pagnell. This is now disproved. (Author's collection, ©Adèle Emm)

Bakers made bread, rolls and biscuits; a confectioner made cakes and pastries although it was common, like Caleb, for small bakeries to produce both. Many a baker also provided the important community function of cooking Sunday and Christmas dinner for poor families without ovens. Even over Christmas, wood-fired ovens were kept hot because it took too long to get an oven up to the correct temperature; a baker might as well earn a penny or two more. In summer, poor families asked the baker to cook their food as it cost more to light the range than pay the baker a penny.

In order for bread to be bought by customers starting work early in the morning, a baker worked overnight mixing and kneading dough, letting it rise again before baking it in the oven. A working day of over eighteen hours was not unusual and it was hard physical work hefting 20 stone hessian sacks of flour.

The Book of Trades 1806 explains how journeymen started at eleven at night making bread rolls with milk, not water, for sale in the morning. There was no method of regulating the oven's heat; it was down to the baker's skill. A bale of burning wood was placed in the oven, the door closed and the baker waited until the wood had burnt to embers. At this point, the burning ash was scraped out and the bread placed on the oven floor using a long-handled *peel*, an implement similar to a shovel and used from the Middle Ages. A water-soaked panel was placed in the doorway to swell in the heat and dough was plastered around the gap to seal it further. Once the dough outside was cooked, it was presumed the bread inside was ready too. As in recipes today, when bread is tapped on the bottom and sounds hollow, it is done. The expression 'the upper crust' comes from here – the base of bread cooked on the oven bottom was burnt black, so the top of the bread, the upper crust, was eaten by the higher social classes.

A fascinating insight into the production of biscuits at the Victualling Office, Deptford, is detailed in the *Book of Trades*. This was a large bakery with twelve wood burning stoves each making bread for 2,040 people, a total of 24,480 people a day – a huge enterprise and surely a precursor of factory manufacturing. A machine mixed the flour and water dough, after which a workman apportioned it between five bakers. Although the biscuits were made by hand, the operation was a slick juggling trick; the first baker formed biscuits two at a time, the second stamped them before throwing them to a third who split them down the middle and slid them under the hand of number four, who tossed peel over the top. The final baker put them in the oven. Seventy biscuits a minute were made in this fashion and the author was so obviously impressed that he failed to mention how the bakery made so much bread as well. Pay was relatively low at ten shillings a week excluding rent for living with the baker. Compare this to trades receiving three to four shillings a day.

Sanctions for dishonest practices were tough. In 1806, a baker could be pilloried and fined for selling short-weight bread. Because the penalty was so severe, the baker added a 'vantage loaf' – an extra roll or piece of bread – to each order, hence the expression 'baker's dozen'. Adding unauthorised ingredients to a loaf of bread, chalk or bone dust for instance, resulted in humiliation around the streets and ultimate expulsion from the livery company. At the time, bread was two types, white (wheaten) and household (cheaper) and had to be clearly labelled as such or, again, the baker was fined. As profit margins were so narrow, skulduggery was common.

When Sunday working was illegal, there was a potential problem with bread availability on Monday. The Bread Act of 1821 permitted London bakers within ten miles of the Royal Exchange to work on Sunday until 1.30am and make deliveries. By 1836, bakers countrywide could work Sunday. Why were these laws so important? Bread was the staple food and for centuries people ate a loaf of bread each day; the baker was a busy man! In 1871, just over 59,000 bakers were recorded in the census.

For centuries, the price of bread was fixed and people sometimes rioted when prices rose, like coal miners in the 1831 Merthyr Rising. Incidentally, this was the first time a red flag, the symbol of the working class, was hoisted. In 1919, after the bread subsidy was removed following the end of the First World War, the cost of a two-pound loaf rose to eight pence and people complained to local newspapers like the *Stockport Advertiser*. Although Stockport shops could charge less, I doubt they did…

The history of baking can be found on the Worshipful Company of Bakers' website at **www.bakers.co.uk**, although there is little on individual bakers. Their motto 'Praise God for all' was the traditional grace before meals. First mentioned in the Pipe Rolls of 1155, this guild is the second oldest and nineteenth in the order of preference. The Bakers' Company does not answer genealogical questions but their records are accessible at London Guildhall.

The volunteer-run database of Sugar Bakers and Sugar Refiners at **www.mawer.clara.net/intro.html** may be of interest. This includes a map of sugar refineries, information about each one and census lists of anyone involved in the industry. The database throws up interesting snippets, such as the fact that a Manchester sugar refiner, Alfred Fryer, started life as a tea dealer and by the 1861 census employed 170 men in his new enterprise. Should your ancestor have lived nearby, he may have been working at this refinery, which provided sugar for the baking, confectionery, drink industries and shops. See Brian Mawer's excellent book on Sugar Bakers for information on working conditions and hazards. It was common in early nineteenth century London for the destitute to sleep outside a sugar bakery where they could get a vestige of warmth.

For anyone with connections to J. Lyons, the corner-house teashop and bakery, the electronic history of the company at **www.kzwp.com/lyons** compiled by Peter Bird might be of interest. It tells the history of the company, information on subsidiaries and, for the genealogist, a list of war dead and memorials plus recent obituaries and people's roles within the company. The list of extended biographies is of more use as the pensioners list is merely that; a name, date of death and for which department they worked. There is also an explanation of the bakery production process, providing background information for anyone whose relative worked here.

Copies of the magazine *The Baker*, published from 1954, can be ordered from the British Library. For John Hearfield's interesting personal approach on the relationship between the price of bread and income in the seventeenth and eighteenth centuries see **www.johnhearfield.com/History/Breadt.htm**. For mills and millwrights, consider Reading-based volunteer-run The Mills Archive at **www.millsarchivetrust.org**. Their search engine is free but for more information, you must become a friend of the trust.

Butchers

It is easy even now to tell a medieval market square; the roads leading towards it are relatively wide to accommodate the chaos of cattle, pigs and sheep driven down to be sold or slaughtered. Until the formation of the railways, all animals by necessity were brought to market live, which could mean driving them distances of up to a hundred miles, during which time they lost a lot of weight.

Stallholders set up according to where they were designated; hawkers and peddlers mingled with customers and butchers erected stalls in the shambles. The hullabaloo from the lowing, bleating and squealing as animals were slaughtered must have been deafening and indeed the Yorkshire Butchers' guild suggests they were the original City executioners. Health, safety and hygiene were non-existent so blood, guts and offal were discarded where they fell, hence the modern meaning of the expression 'a shambles'. The word originates from Anglo Saxon *scamel* meaning 'bench', in other words the benches or blocks where butchers set up their stalls, slaughtered the animals and displayed the meat for sale. Although shambles had disappeared in our market towns by the mid-1800s (the only surviving example can be found in Shepton Mallet), the name still appears in York, Manchester, Worcester and Stroud, among others. It is no coincidence that York Shambles is on a hill; blood could run down and away.

The legendary heart of the industry, London's Smithfield Market **www.smithfieldmarket.com**, at almost ten acres, is the largest wholesale meat market in the UK and one of the largest in Europe, although at the time of writing there was a discussion about its survival. The market itself is over 140 years old but for over 800 years there has been a livestock market on this site with records showing horses, pigs and cattle were sold here from 1174. Following the Sunday Observance Act of 1672, butchers were prohibited from killing or selling meat on the Sabbath.

From 1133 to 1855, Bartholomew Fair was staged at Smithfield every August, moving to September from 1753. St Bartholomew's Church the Great (founded 1123) and St Bartholomew's Hospital still stand nearby. It was at Smithfield in 1381 that Wat Tyler, leader of the Peasants' Revolt, met Richard II and was stabbed and died from his wounds. During the reign of Mary Tudor, 200 Protestants were burnt here for their religious beliefs.

Smithfield was transformed following the formation of the railway network and its own station. By 1849, one million animals arrived at Smithfield by train as carcasses having been slaughtered elsewhere. Smithfield had its own alcohol licensing laws, opening at 5.30 am after a hard night's butchering, but originally only people working at the market could drink in its taverns.

During the frost fair of 1814 when the Thames froze over for five days, one enterprising butcher roasted a sheep, marketing it as 'Lapland mutton'.

The butcher's hey-day was after the Industrial Revolution when Britain was the richest country in the world. The massive rise in population and prosperity meant a consequently dramatic increase in meat consumption. Once refrigeration was available from the mid-1800s, the butcher could both slaughter and store meat and thus the butcher's shop was born. Up to that point, meat was a fast-turn-round comestible; the only methods of preservation were salting, smoking, curing or drying. Meat was butchered in the slaughterhouse then kept away from it.

Once an animal was dead, the butcher prepared the carcass, slicing it in half, eviscerating, chopping into different cuts, boning and trimming using tools such as block, cleaver, saws, hooks (for hanging), knives and leather or whetstones to sharpen them. Old cookery books show cuts for different animals, or view demonstrations on **www.eblextrade.co.uk/videos**. The butcher was recognisable by his white apron, bloodied of course, and, more recently, dark blue striped apron and straw boater.

On the high street, the butcher displayed carcasses outside his shop and produced foodstuffs such as sausages, often to secret, handed-down recipes. It was not uncommon for butchers to have a secondary occupation; pub owner and landlord was popular, with the slaughterhouse behind the bar. Many butchers, like other tradesmen, lived above the shop.

There was a Butchers' Hall in Farringdon outside London's walls as early as 975, although the Worshipful Company of Butchers **www.butchershall.com** didn't receive its Arms until 1540. Other

Meat hanging in Barbecoa Butchery near St Paul's Cathedral. (©Adèle Emm)

cities such as York **http://yorkbutchersgild.weebly.com** had guilds, but genealogical information is scanty. Concerned with the slaughter of horses and cattle, the Knackers Act of 1786 required slaughter house keepers to be licenced annually by Quarter Sessions. The penalty for infraction was a fine, imprisonment and 'publick or private whipping'. If registers, order books or certificates survive, they will be in the local record offices. Durham, for instance, has some order books for 1881–94. The *Meat Trades' Journal and Cattle Salesman's Gazette* has been published by Reed since 1888; the British Library has copies.

Costermongers, Pedlars and Hawkers

Costermonger is thought to derive from 'costard,' a type of apple; in other words, an apple seller. It is unlikely that a family historian can trace much about these itinerant salesmen apart from names in the census and court records for misdemeanours. An interesting description of their lives is, however, found in the fascinating but quirky *Palace and Hovel or Phases of London Life* by American traveller Daniel Joseph Kirwan, published in 1870 and found online at **https://archive.org/stream/palacehovel00kirw**.

The book is written like a penny dreadful, with attempts at translating cockney vernacular and rhyming slang (derived from the contraction of 'secret' and 'lang') for an American to get a flavour of Victorian London. For anyone with London ancestors or an interest in the past, it is a wonderfully evocative narrative and, in a style rivalling Dickens, Chapter IX explains the life of a London costermonger. We learn (p392) that costermongers earned about fifteen to twenty shillings in a good week, but in winter when vegetables were scarce, less than eight shillings for the same work and hours. Their wages had to cover the trading licence which, according to Kirwan, was £4 or £5 per year, and also, of course, the merchandise. Even with a licence, they must keep moving or incur the hostility of the local shopkeepers, who saw them as riffraff and rivals, although social researcher Charles Booth (1840–1916) explained that small shopkeepers were not averse to buying from costermongers themselves. Kirwan aptly describes these itinerant tradesmen plying their wares from a cart as having 'a loud vocation' and to make a living, they needed charisma. On p393, Kirwan lists the numbers and types of shop in different London areas. A description of markets in the 1860s including Smithfield and Covent Garden is found from p435 and Billingsgate Fish Market from p508.

In the nineteenth century, costermongers sewed mother-of-pearl buttons found in the street along the seams of their trousers and as 'flashes' in their caps – the origin of pearly kings and queens.

Pedlars were itinerants peddling from a backpack, not a barrow or cart. A 'ped', according to Brewer's *Dictionary of Phrase and Fable* was their backpack. Hawkers and pedlars had to be licensed, temporarily at first, from 1697. These licences were extended and are explained on a National Archives site at **http://discovery.national archives.gov.uk/SearchUI/details?Uri=C9389**. Any licences still existing are held at local record offices. From the 1820s, pedlars and hawkers were discouraged from trading in towns and cities outside London and the necessary licence was too expensive for the majority to trade legally. In the 1871 census, it is estimated that there were 45,000 pedlars and hawkers and a lucky few became household names. Moshe Osinsky, a Jewish Lithuanian refugee, arrived in Manchester in 1900 and metamorphosed himself into Sir Montague Burton of suit and tailoring fame. Marks and Spencer is a similar story. Some pedlars and hawkers hailed from Romany stock and the Romany and Traveller Family History Society **http://rtfhs.org.uk** might be useful.

Drapers

The draper was a mainstay of the high street. When most women made their own clothes or had them made, the draper sold the material whilst the haberdasher sold buttons, thread, needles, trimmings, ribbons and frills. Eventually it became common for the draper to sell everything. In the 1871 census, there were 74,337 drapers 'linen and wool', 25,000 up from 1851.

The word draper comes from old French *draper*, to weave or drape; *drap* was cloth (in modern French it is used to mean 'sheet', as for a bed). The importance of cloth is reinforced by the number of important medieval cloth halls throughout Europe, for example in Krakow (Poland), Ypres (Belgium), and our own Leeds. Although the main stock was cloth, they also sold leather and imported goods such as spices.

From the fifteenth century, wool was crucial to our national wealth and you only have to see the size of some churches in East Anglia to appreciate its importance. The Drapers' Company was extremely wealthy, although various laws needed to be passed to protect the industry. In 1551 Edward VI passed an act to bring down the price of wool by ensuring only merchants could buy it. From 1666 to 1680, the Burying in Woollen Acts made it compulsory for corpses to be buried in woollen shrouds unless they had died of plague or were destitute. For the family historian this means that at burial, an affidavit appears next to the registry entry to prove this had happened. The penalty was a £5 fine – an enormous sum. For those without the wherewithal to pay, the corpse was buried naked, also recorded in the register. Cotton was imported from the late seventeenth century by the East India Company.

In London the medieval drapers' trade was governed by the Worshipful Company of Drapers **www.thedrapers.co.uk**, third in the Great Twelve Livery Companies. The annual Cloth Fair took place in the Smithfield area of London from the twelfth century until 1855. The Drapers' first Royal Charter was granted in 1364, although records show there had been an informal fraternity since 1180. The wealthier members were merchants, the more lowly ran shops.

The Drapers' emblem, the Golden Fleece, is prominent on the current Drapers' Hall (see photo in Chapter 2) featuring on the coat of arms above the helmet and as a motif on members' ties. Archives are held at Drapers' Hall and the website details what they hold. For family history purposes, it is essential to check your draper was a member via the Records of London's Livery Company Online (ROLLCO) at **www.londonroll.org** before contacting them. Should you be lucky enough to find an ancestor, contact the Company. Researchers are admitted by appointment to the archives at the discretion of the Company, but undertake their own research. The details will not reveal personal or business information about the draper. *A History of the Company of the Worshipful Company of Drapers* by Rev A.H. Johnson covers its history up to the fifteenth century and can be found online at **http://archive.org/stream/historyof worship04johnuoft/historyofworship04johnuoft_djvu.txt**.

Percival Boyd (1866–1955, of Boyd's Marriage Index) was also responsible for Boyd's Inhabitants of London found online on FindMyPast. Within this are families of the Drapers' Company.

Boyd's Inhabitants of London is also useful for family units dating from the sixteenth to the early twentieth centuries of which, contrary to the name, only a third were London based.

There were other drapers' guilds throughout the country, in Coventry, Shrewsbury, and Durham for example. The Shropshire Record Office has fully catalogued substantial records for the Shrewsbury Drapers' Company, searchable on their website via Searching our Collections/ Discovering Shropshire's History. There are two main sections; administrative (apprentice papers, admissions, petitions, rentals) and property deeds, with a wealth of information about individuals if you are lucky enough to have someone recorded there.

Coventry's Drapers' Hall is relatively new, having been built in 1831–32, although a Drapers' Company existed at least a century before its official records began in 1534. Records include, inter alia, Fellowship of Drapers membership records and indentures from 1720–1850 and records for other trades. Unfortunately, without Latin and palaeographical skills, many records are hard to decipher. There is an extensive catalogue. The Durham guild archives are at Durham University **http://reed.dur.ac.uk/xtf/view?docId=ead/adm/dcg.xml** which holds records for the eighteenth and nineteenth centuries.

The Drapers' Company, like many others, built almshouses and you may find that your ancestors lived in these. John Pemel left £1,200 in his 1681 will for the Company to buy land and Pemel's almshouses were duly built in Southwark in 1698, where four widows of the Freemen and four widows of Stepney seamen could be housed, clothed and given coals.

Record offices' catalogues may reveal useful nuggets, such as in Cambridgeshire, where draper Henry Martin takes a lease in August 1869 for four years for a shop and house in Newmarket All Saints at an annual rent of £82. Local newspapers may be useful.

Fishmongers

We all believe fish was eaten on Fridays, holy days and during Lent for religious reasons, but this isn't strictly accurate. Henry VIII eschewed fish with the consequence that the fish industry significantly deteriorated during his reign. Hoping to reverse the decline by encouraging people to eat more fish, his son, Edward VII, passed a law in 1548–49 making it mandatory to fast from meat on Friday and Saturday. Of course, those too poor to eat meat found it just as hard to eat fish, especially if they lived some way from the coast, so their regular fare of vegetables was supplemented by poaching (possibly fish…). For large city dwellers or those near the coast and rivers, fish was comparatively available; the 1851 census for Newport Pagnell, a town pretty much as far from the sea as could be, records two fishermen.

An old maxim recommends never buying fish on Monday. Billingsgate Market is closed on Sundays and Mondays and fishing boats didn't land on Sundays, so fish would be stale. Sunday fishing for salmon and sea trout is still illegal in Scotland. In 1762, the Fish Carriage Act permitted fish carts to travel around the country on Sundays and a century later the Billingsgate Act 1868 permitted the sale of mackerel on Sunday. How far the fish had come was a serious consideration when buying, as before refrigeration fish was packed in ice boxes and difficult to keep frozen.

Fish was unloaded at Billingsgate and Queenhithe in London. Although it moved to Canary Wharf in 1982, Billingsgate has been in existence since at least the sixteenth century. Prior to then, Edward III granted a charter in 1327 prohibiting nearby rival markets. From 1699 until 2012, porters carrying fish crates needed a licence to work here. They famously wore leather hats, 'bobbers', based on headgear worn by archers in battles such as Agincourt (1415), flat at the top where fish crates rested, channels in the brims collecting blood and effluent.

A major function of the Company of Fishmongers **www. fishhall.org.uk** was to inspect the quality and freshness of fish in Billingsgate. It received its first Royal Charter in about 1272, making it among the oldest London guilds; its importance was proven by ranking fourth in the Twelve Great Livery Companies. Up to the fifteenth century, it had the monopoly of fish sales in London with a tax levied on every box of fish sold. Fishmongers Hall was one of the first buildings destroyed in the Great Fire, but the chest containing the records, company silver and its money were saved. The current hall, constructed in 1835 next to London Bridge, was damaged during the Blitz but has been fully restored. Unlike others, tours are open to the general public. Their records are at Guildhall.

Victorian Daniel Kirwan in *Palace and Hovel* writes about the London experience of fish and fishing **https://archive.org/stream/ palacehovel00kirw#page/510/mode/2up**, including the tonnage of fish brought in from the various ports around Britain, Billingsgate Fish Market and the cost and prices fishermen could get for their catch. The fish merchants were the first to buy; the remainder was sold to costermongers. Page 517 gives statistics for the amounts and types of fish sold in the 1860s; a very different picture to today when fish is flown around the world.

London fishmongers bought sprats, cod, eels, plaice, whiting, herring and mackerel from Billingsgate, taking it to their shops where they might smoke or dry mackerel and herring for a longer shelf life. Before refrigeration, their ice supply was delivered in large blocks by the ice cart and kept in the 'ice cupboard'.

Fishmongers elsewhere bought produce from local fishermen who caught fish in the rivers or collected it from the nearest fish dock or train from Hull, Lowestoft, Grimsby, North Shields, Aberdeen and the like. The fish supplied was that day's catch from local waters so there was limited choice. It was a long, dirty day; early morning buying and collecting fish, preparing and selling it and cleaning up afterwards. The fishmonger business increased with better preservation techniques and the proliferation of the railway system; the fish train was a common sight. In 1851, census records show 10,439 listing it as their occupation. By 1871, it was 14,880. A fishmonger has traded at the same place on Bridge Street Brow near Stockport market for over 160 years.

Greengrocers/Fruiterers

Prior to Victoria's reign, fruit and vegetables were expensive so people grew their own, foraged for seasonal produce such as fruit, wild berries, mushrooms, leaves and such like or, if they couldn't afford to buy them, did without.

The high-street greengrocer sourced his own produce and, before air-freight and better road transport, it was local and seasonal. Produce was transported by cart or railway; the daily seasonal watercress train transporting cress from Hampshire to customers in London is an example. My father remembers his mother's despair at winter vegetables in 1920s Dukinfield being merely cabbage and potatoes. The improvement in transport and readier availability of fruit and vegetables is shown in the census records; there were 14,320 greengrocer/fruiterers in 1851, but by 1871 this had increased to 25,819.

Greengrocers displayed their wares piled both outside and inside the shop. Some had a reputation for putting the freshest and tastiest at the top whilst selling bruised ones from the back to the unsuspecting customer. Unlike today, customers were discouraged from touching or choosing the produce.

Grocers

Emphasising its importance, the Worshipful Company of Grocers **www.grocershall.co.uk** is second in the order of preference and a member of the Great Twelve City Livery Companies. It dates back to 1180 as the Ancient Guild of Pepperers in the Pipe Rolls (the written records of the king's exchequer accounts and held in the National Archives) and referred to as the Company of Grossers (produce was sold gross) from 1373. The first hall, built in 1428, was, like most other halls in London, destroyed in the Great Fire. The fifth and current hall was built in 1970. Their records are held at Guildhall. Grocers were highly skilled at preparing foodstuffs for selling in the shop. They might, for instance, cook their own hams (sixpence a quarter pound in 1911) and bag dry goods such as tea, flour, sugar, dried fruit and spices into smaller quantities. Butter and cheese was cut to size; cheese from the wheel (offering a taste to the customer) and butter formed into pats from larger blocks, often salted by the grocer himself. Everything was weighed, sliced (bacon) and sold accordingly. Thrifty householders saved glass jars and bottles and returned them for refilling with, for instance, jams and pickles.

Grocers' importance on the high street is reflected in their burgeoning numbers; in 1851, there were just short of 86,000, but by 1871 there were just over 111,000, coinciding with the increase in the factory system and longer working hours. Household names such as Fortnum and Mason (1707) and Sainsbury (1869) started out as grocers. Sainsbury's archive, holding over 16,000 documents, photographs and objects, is at the Museum of London. There are some staff records.

The Grocer magazine has been published since 1862 by William Reed (1830–1920), a farmer's son who worked as a sugar merchant before setting up his eponymous publishing company, still in existence and still family owned. This company also published titles for industries such as the brewing and tobacco trade. Although *The Grocer* may not be useful for family historians, it shows how trade has changed, offering a fascinating insight into the grocery business over the years. Copies for 1862–86 and for 1886–1942 when it changed its title to *The Grocer and Oil Trade Review* are held at the British Library. It needs to be pre-ordered as it takes forty-eight hours to get to the St Pancras reading rooms. Other libraries holding copies are the Universities of Cambridge, Oxford and Nottingham and the National Libraries of Scotland and Wales, but check which copies they hold.

Haberdashers

Jane Austen's aunt, Jane Cholmeley Leigh Perrot, was accused of shoplifting a card of white lace from Elizabeth Gregory's Bath milliner/haberdashers in August 1799. At her trial, a plan of the shop was produced showing the position of the compter (counter), the desk and display of goods by the Style Street window. Austen's aunt was acquitted.

According to Brewer, haberdasher comes from *hapertas*, a cloth the width of which was settled by Magna Charta (sic). A *hapertas-er* is the seller of hapertas-erie.' The high street's haberdasher sold sewing articles; beads, needles, thread, bobbins, gloves, ribbons, pins, toys and the like. Like Miss Gregory's emporium, they occasionally doubled as milliners or drapers, measured out material and trimmings and advised as style guru on clothing and colours.

The London Company of Haberdashers **www.haberdashers.co.uk** is eighth in the Great Twelve Livery Companies, one below Merchant Taylors and Skinners. They were in existence before the first written record in the Mayor's Court of 1371 and were mentioned in Chaucer's (c.1345–1400) *Canterbury Tales* as Hurrers, the haberdasher's precursor who sold gentlemen's clothing and accessories, hats, gloves and women's millinery. In 1502 the haberdashers merged with the hatmakers' fraternity. By 1650, London was too big for the Company to control the haberdashery trade so it turned its attention to education and charity such as the Haberdasher schools, with which it is still involved. Its records are held at Guildhall Library.

Ironmongers

An ironmonger sold anything made of metal; tools and hardware alongside household implements such as brooms, candles and kitchen utensils – their sign was a dog with its head in a pot. Some made small metal items and candles. The Worshipful Company of Ironmongers **www.ironmongers.org**, originally Ferroners, (Latin *fer* meaning iron), received its Charter in 1463, although it had been in existence since at least 1300 when records show members taking action against the smiths of the Weald over the quality of iron supplied for wheels. Tenth in the order of precedence, its coat of arms shows various metal implements and two salamanders as crests; these creatures were believed to survive fire. Its motto, *Assher dure*, is a phonetic rendering of French *acier dure* meaning 'steel is hard' and used by the Ironmongers Company since the Royal Charter.

Ironmongers Hall coat of arms, London. (©Adèle Emm)

Bennetts in Derby, established under the name Weatherhead Walters & Company in 1734 as an ironmonger at 8 Iron Gate, regards itself as the world's first department store. At 11 Iron Gate in the 1851 census, Widower Samuel Weatherhead (born c.1784) employed eight men, three apprentices and two servants.

The oldest ironmonger's shop in London was established as Preslands in 1797 at 493–495 Hackney Road, having been founded in around 1760 as a carriage and coachbuilders on the same site. In the 1890s it became W.H. Clark and there are plenty of pictures on the internet showing how it used to look. Closed now and very bedraggled, the building is, at the time of writing, still there.

W.H. Clark's, Ironmonger, Hackney Road, London. Unaltered for over two hundred years, its Georgian heritage can clearly be seen above the shop front. My shoemaking relatives living in nearby Minerva Street c.1836 to 1911 would have walked past this shop every day. Opening as Preslands in 1797, it closed in 2013. (©Adèle Emm)

The oldest hat shop in the world is Lock & Co. in St James Street, London, established 1676. One of the oldest family-owned businesses, it is where the bowler hat, the banker's symbol, was developed by James Lock in 1850 for his client, William Coke, Earl of Leicester. Lock is not a hat maker (see Chapter 9) and holds no records of past staff. Business records are held at London Metropolitan Archives.

Lock's Hat Shop, St James' Street, London, established 1676. (©Adèle Emm)

A similarly family owned specialist shop is James Smith & Sons in New Oxford Street, London, which has made and sold umbrellas and walking-sticks since 1830. Also a family business, no records are available to the public nor can they answer genealogical questions; Victorian umbrella makers worked for several shops in this vicinity. However, if you are interested in how your ancestors made umbrellas, see their website **www.james-smith.co.uk/history**.

Other time-travel opportunities are: Beamish Open Air Museum in County Durham **www.beamish.org.uk**; Lark Hill Place at Salford Museum **www.salfordcommunityleisure.co.uk/culture/salford-museum-and-art-gallery/lark-hill-place**; Blists Hill Victorian Town, Ironbridge, Shropshire **www.ironbridge.org.uk/our-attractions/blists-hill-victorian-town** and York Castle Museum's Kirkgate **www.kirkgatevictorianstreet.org.uk/home.html** among others. The School of Artisan Food in Mansfield **www.school ofartisanfood.org** runs courses on non-industrialised methods of producing bread, cheese and butchery which may be of interest.

Chapter 6
BUILDERS AND THE BUILDING TRADE

London Bridge is falling down, falling down,
Build it up with sticks and stones, sticks and stones,
Build it up with wood and clay,
Build it up with stone so strong...
traditional nursery rhyme dating from the Middle Ages

Standing proud on the skyline of our towns and cities as a testament to the skill of our ancestors are cathedrals, some over a thousand years old and built with rudimentary scaffolding and without cranes or JCBs. The labourers working in the shadow of Wren, Bazalgette, Hawksmoor and Brunel, all the way back to the Romans, are unknown, but the engineering projects: railways, viaducts, stations, tunnels and bridges, Hadrian's Wall, Georgian mansions and terraces are their legacy.

The issue for tracing your ancestors who worked on great Victorian projects and the buildings that surround us is that there are hardly any records available. Surviving wage books held at record offices may not mention workmen by name and those that do are under the name of the firm for whom they worked.

The Parliamentary Archives **www.portcullis.parliament.uk/ calmview** for the New Houses of Parliament in the nineteenth and twentieth centuries are in the Palace of Westminster. Few records relate to men working on the building, although there are records of companies given contracts and held at the National Archives. For anyone working on the Clock Tower, the company awarded the contract was Edward John Dent, which still exists; their historical records are held at Guildhall.

The Builder, published in London and founded in 1842 by Joseph Hansom (1803–82) of Hansom cab fame, is an architectural and building periodical also exploring housing and social contexts. By1833, under editor George Godwin, it was the foremost journal for the building industry. Some architects, artists, craftsmen and engineers are mentioned by name and the journal was indexed annually from 1842–79, with half-yearly indexes from 1880. Some copies are held at the LMA; order in advance. The British Library has volumes from 1842 onwards.

For those tracing ancestors working outside the metropolis, the task is often even more onerous. Trawling through record offices for the area, name and profession is the best bet. With perseverance, you may strike lucky. A further consideration is that, in the 1871 census for instance, 516,605 people were recorded as labourers, who could have worked in anything from agriculture, factories, engineering and building supporting masons, bricklayers, blacksmiths and railways…

Auctioneers and House Agents

Although slaves were sold by auction during the Roman era, auctions were relatively rare until 'sales by the candle' (Chapter 9) operating from the fifteenth century. Auctions as we know them began roughly in the seventeenth century with art auctions in coffeehouses followed by antiquities (Sotheby's 1744, Christie's 1766, Bonhams 1793).

Unlike other trades and artisans in this chapter, auctioneers and house agents weren't manual workers, but were in the business of selling land, property and contents, receiving either a fee or percentage of the transaction. In existence from the mid-eighteenth century and certainly before the 1841 census (auctioneers Rowley, Son and Royce operated in the Cambridge area before the 1830s) they were relatively rare; Henry Kent's London directory of 1738 and 1754 (found online through a Google search for Kent's Original London Directory) lists none.

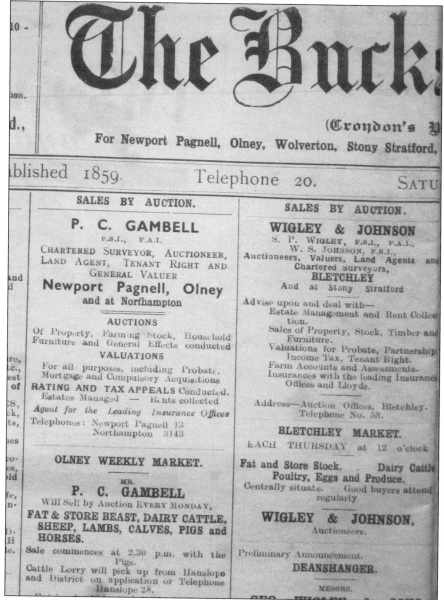

Auctioneers' advertisements on the front page of The Buck's Standard, *18 June 1938. (Author's collection)*

A reason for including auctioneers in this book is because their records hold a plethora of information about so many other trades. Depending on why the auction took place: bankruptcy, death or stipulations in a will, inventories itemised everything sold including for example blacksmith's tools, an area of land for sale in poles, perches and furlongs, crops in a field, furniture in a house, bedding and clothing – all found in the auctioneers' ledgers. The auction took place at the property or a nearby inn and flyers are often included among the archives.

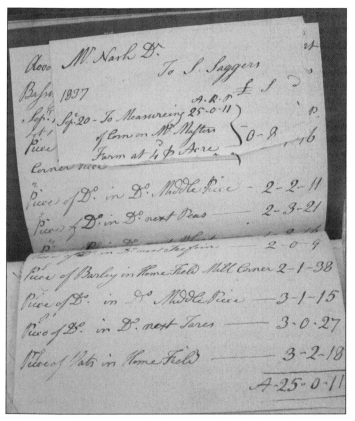

Rowley Son and Royce auctioneer's itemised bill for measuring and valuing crops in Mr Masters' field, September 1837. Total £25 0 11. (Courtesy Cambridgeshire Archives 296/B759)

The seller paid the auctioneers' expenses from the proceeds. For Rowley, Son and Royce that might include the cost of posting bills, distributing catalogues, the town crier (one shilling) and advertising in the newspaper (sixteen shillings). Even in 1822, auctioneers were not averse to giving credit, although requiring a joint note of security, a deposit of twenty per cent payable on the day of the sale and the final balance due on a quarter day such as 24 December.

For accounts and books still existing (Discovery is useful), go to the relevant record office where ledgers, bound and written in meticulous copperplate, hold the itemised inventories and accounts. The signatures of officiating agents and clients, perhaps your ancestor, are a bonus.

An estate agent managed rents, leases and property for landowners and was salaried. In 1730, Richard Andrews was the estate agent/steward for the London Grosvenor Estate and was paid £80 a year. His son, Robert, originally a solicitor, also acted as land agent to the Grosvenors and when he died in 1763 was receiving £150 per annum.

Bricklayers

According to *The Book of Trades* 1806 a bricklayer working in London tiled, paved and built walls and chimneys. To survive in the countryside where jobs were few, he was more versatile, occasionally dabbling in stone masonry and plastering, a trade in itself especially when exposed brick was unpopular, as during the Renaissance. Sounding like a careers advice booklet, it explains tools: brick trowel, saw, brick axe, plumb lines, square, level and ten-foot measuring rod and materials: bricks, tiles, mortar, nails and lathes. Bricklayers were not expected to supply bricks. Their labourers made mortar from lime and the duo was expected to lay a thousand bricks a day. At four to five shillings and sixpence a day, the journeyman bricklayer earned less than other trades. His labourer received between half a crown (two shillings and sixpence) and three shillings and sixpence a day. Because a bricklayer calculated estimates for the job and included scaffolding – more health and safety conscious than we would have expected – he was both numerate and literate. Removing rubbish was extra. Digging wells was charged by the foot on a sliding scale; deeper wells were more expensive. Soil dispersal was extra.

Massive building projects from the mid-1800s created a shortage of skilled labour, including bricklayers, especially as bricks were cheaper than stone. These projects included Sir Joseph Bazalgette's (1819–91) plans for building 1,300 miles of sewers beneath London to prevent cholera epidemics, the London Embankment and the railway network. The Midland Grand Hotel at St Pancras, which opened in 1868, cost an enormous £438,000 to build. Wages rose. In 1865, bricklayers were earning six shillings and sixpence a day. For those working in 1871 on the Chelsea Embankment, a shilling bonus a day was added with labourers earning sixpence more. Bricklayers on these projects were merely subcontractors laying bricks supplied by London Brickworks. The censuses highlight the burgeoning building projects; in 1851, 67,989 bricklayers were recorded and two decades later, nearly 100,000.

Brickmakers

When the Romans left, Britain returned to former materials of timber, stone, flint and cob (clay and straw found in old Devon houses). Bricks, generally from the Low Countries, were reintroduced around the twelfth century but only became fashionable, for those with money, after the fabulous Tudor palaces such as Hampton Court were built.

Brickmaking requires clay and sand, so brick makers worked where clay was abundant and easily obtainable, such as in the marls of Buckinghamshire and Bedfordshire. For a history of the London Brick Company in Stewartby, follow the links on **www. bedfordshire.gov.uk**. In Kent, it is estimated that one in five of the male population were working in the brickfields at one time.

Brickmaking requires a plentiful supply of water – clay needs

Bricks at Ashford in Kent dating from 1630. English bond. Alternate courses of stretcher and header. (©Adèle Emm)

Cambridge: Flemish bond, stretcher and header overlapping. These bricks date from 1754, prior to the 1784 brick tax. (©Adèle Emm)

Common/American bond bricks in Stockport, dating from around 1824. Five or six courses of stretcher between courses of header. The brick tax was removed in 1850. (©Adèle Emm)

moisture to be turned into bricks. Physically dug out of the ground in autumn, clay was left to weather over winter. In spring, the clay was broken up, stones removed, water and sand added and it was kneaded by men or animals into a paste. Lumps were knocked out. Hunks of clay were rolled in sand to prevent it sticking and hurled with force into a brick mould (bigger than the subsequent brick as they shrink in the kiln) to remove air pockets. A wire, like a cheese wire, cut excess clay from the top of the mould, sand was sprinkled on the top of the brick, a wooden board was placed on top and the mould inverted to release the brick, which was stacked and dried before firing in a kiln. It took at least a day for the brick to cool down. The type of clay, its colour and iron content predetermined the final colour of the brick although they could be dyed.

It was hard physical seasonal work making at least 5,000 bricks a day in wet, damp conditions and, although it was comparatively well paid, another occupation was needed during the 'off season'. In 1784, a Brick Tax was introduced at four shillings a thousand. By 1805, the tax was nearly six shillings a thousand and bricks were made larger to compensate. Of course, the government became wise to this and in 1806, when *The Book of Trades* was published, an Act of Parliament specified the size of a brick at 8½ inches long, 2½ inches thick and 4 inches wide. After abolition in 1850, houses were more likely to be built of brick, but not before some brickmakers had gone out of business and others had resorted to expensive brickmaking machines which, accordingly, they continued to use. Once made, prior to the railways, bricks were transported to the building project by cart or barge.

Rev David Cufley has compiled a brickmaker's index mainly for England but with some Scottish brickmakers; **http://cufley.co.uk/ brkindx.htm**. The index is not available to the general public and you will need to contact him via his website. A bibliography of books dealing with brickmaking is on **http://cufley.co.uk/ brckbook.htm**.

Unknown carpenter/joiner holding saw. Studio photo from family album, date unknown. The purpose of the folded apron is also unknown. Research has been inconclusive. (Author's collection, ©Adèle Emm)

Carpenters, Joiners, Turners and Sawyers

According to *The Book of Trades* 1806, the carpenter's craft was installing rafters, beams and joists into property, whereas the joiner made doors, door frames, wainscoting and sashes for windows, although both trades were often interchangeable. The type of wood and its source such as deal (fir), oak, elm and mahogany is described as well as tools required: saws, planes, chisels, hammers, gimlets etc. Workmen owned their tools which, when the book was written, cost

Toolbox made c.1905 by William Edgar Emms during his apprenticeship. He worked as a coachbuilder but making a toolbox was standard practice in similar trades. (©Adèle Emm)

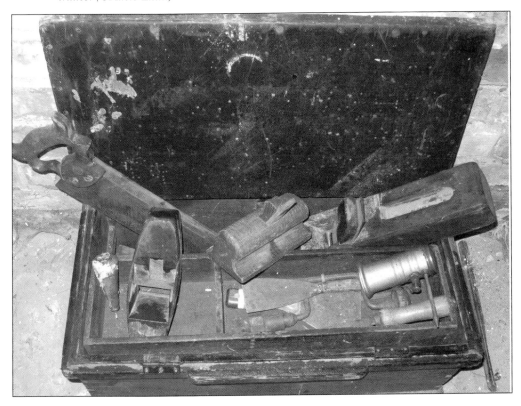

£20 or more. Considering the weekly wage of a journeyman carpenter was between three shillings and sixpence and four shillings and sixpence, this was a hefty investment. One of the first things an apprentice made was his toolbox and many, kept for sentimental reasons, turn up at auctions.

A sad task for the small village carpenter was to act as undertaker and make the coffins; for the poor, a basic box.

Wood turners have operated lathes since at least Egyptian times when it required two men, one turning the wood with a rope while the other carved it into bowls, platters, spindles, furniture legs and so on. In medieval times, the master carved while the apprentice turned the crank to turn the wood. The term 'bodger' comes from a wood-turner buying a plot of land and turning all the trees into chair

Old sawmill, Dunham Park (now Dunham Massey), from postcard dated 1909. (Author's collection, © Adèle Emm)

and table legs. Because he only made part of the furniture, the term came to mean someone who couldn't do or finish a job properly.

The invention of the saw is mythically accredited to Icarus, he of the flying-too-close-to-the-sun fame who used a fish bone as saw. A painting in Herculaneum shows an early example of a saw pit. To learn how saws were made, see *The Book of Trades*. In a traditional saw pit, one man stands above the tree-trunk whilst his mate saws the trunk in the pit beneath, wedges holding open the fissures as they worked. The rate of pay for such strenuous work was twelve to eighteen shillings a day, a veritable fortune. During the Industrial Revolution, which saw an increasing demand for wood by carpenters and joiners, the mill took much of the strain out of the job. Working examples of saw mills are found throughout the country including Dunham Massey (National Trust) near Altrincham, powered by water. Anybody whose ancestors worked on the Whitbread Estate as a sawyer might find information on the management in the records held at Bedfordshire county library. If your sawyer ancestor worked on an estate, check the local archives.

In London, several guilds oversaw their members, including the Company of Joiners and Ceilers **www.joinersandceilers.co.uk** forty-first in the order of preference; the Company of Turners **www.turnersco.com**, a medieval turner put his mark on the bottom of his work; and the Company of Carpenters **www.thecarpenters company.co.uk**, whose archives are kept at Carpenters' Hall and Guildhall Library/LMA. For a list of what is available from the 1720s see **www.londonlives.org/browse.jsp?archive=CC**, which describes the Carpenters' Minute Books of Courts and Committees and you can view names online. An explanation of the lives of carpenters and apprentices and their tools is on **www.londonlives.org/static/ CarpentersCompany.jsp**.

The Shrewsbury Carpenters Company records are held at the Shropshire Record Centre, which has admissions, lists of freemen and apprentice records for 1538–1854. They also hold records for bricklayers and plasterers.

For union records, the Modern Record Centre has information

from 1895 but you must know the union and branch or you will wade through an awful lot of material. The annual reports of the Amalgamated Society of Carpenters and Joiners/Amalgamated Society of Woodworkers dates from 1860 and contains obituaries of members and their wives, but you'll need the date of death, date of admission and the branch. The centre also holds records for the following:

- Associated Carpenters and Joiners' Society of Scotland, 1863–1911
- General Union of Carpenters and Joiners (earlier the Friendly Society of Operative House Carpenters and Joiners of Great Britain and Ireland), 1845–1921
- Protective Association of Joiners of Glasgow, 1847–61
- Preston Joiners' Society, 1807–39
- Mersey Ship Joiners' Association, 1870–1900

For other records, visit the relevant records offices.

Road Builders and Menders

The beginning of state control of roads was the Highways Act 1555 when the parish was made responsible for road maintenance. This inevitably failed because of the increase in traffic and too little money. A century later, the Highways Act 1663 (**www.british-history.ac.uk/report.aspx?compid=47337**) appointed Justices of the Peace to employ surveyors to repair roads and collect tolls in Hertfordshire, Huntingdonshire and Cambridgeshire; the levy charged was a penny for a horse, sixpence for a coach, a shilling per wagon, eight pence for a cart and tuppence for twenty pigs. Its success led to the Turnpike Act 1707 and numerous Turnpike Trusts setting up and maintaining toll roads countrywide. These were local initiatives requiring individual Acts of Parliament; people paid to use the roads and profits were split between shareholders and road maintenance. The location of English Turnpike Trusts are listed on www.turnpikes.org.uk as well as tollhouses and milestones. Any ancestor living near one could have worked that stretch of road.

McAdam (1756–1836, of tarmacadam fame) and Telford (1757–1834) are credited with developing road building improvements. In 1766, milestones became compulsory on all turnpike roads, and by 1821 there were more than 18,000 miles of turnpike roads in England all requiring labour. Road builders were not necessarily responsible for maintaining wooden bridges which, due to increasing traffic from turnpike roads, were failing and needed to be rebuilt in stone. The ownership of bridges and maintenance fell to regional local government, with separate contracts for maintaining them. The Turnpike Trusts were closed from the 1870s.

The 1851 census listed 10,923 road labourers, but those recorded as general labourers are not included in this figure. Good road builders used the same skills as those of the mason, skilfully cutting stones for paving and crushing stones for aggregate. To save time, money and sweat, they used the stone nearest to hand.

The problem is that, unless they had a specific county contract for, say, maintaining bridges in Bedfordshire, they are unlikely to be named in records. Take Thomas Spurrett (1804–97) of Bampton as an example. My cousin spent hours in Oxford Record Office finally unearthing uncatalogued letters between Thomas and the County Surveyor of Works. Thomas had been caught cheating the county for maintenance he didn't actually do. If you are prepared to put in time at your local record office, you may strike lucky.

Painters

A well-known novel about the life of a housepainter is *The Ragged Trousered Philanthropists* by Robert Tressell, pseudonym of Irish socialist Robert Noonan (1870–1911). Published posthumously, it is a diatribe against the hypocrisy and double standards of Edwardian society, depicting Edwardian working conditions in scathing terms; an interesting read if your ancestor was a house painter and decorator.

The earliest reference to the Worshipful Company of Painter Stainers **www.paintershall.co.uk** in London is 1283 when *payntors* painted everything including using gold; murals, banners, barges and portraits on wood, stone and metal. The *steynors* applied colour to fabric. Some famous artists belonged to the Company including Reynolds, Kneller and Millais. Records are held in London's Guildhall Library. An essay written for his B.A. in 1993 on the history of house painting in London c.1660–1850 by Patrick Baty can be found online via a Google search. In it, he explains, among other things, their working conditions, the paint-shop and how painters made their own paint.

Stone Masons

A stone mason hews and cuts stone and marble into blocks and squares for building and, unlike wood and thatch, there is no room for mistake. Damage to stone is irreversible. The quarryman extracted the stone from the ground, the banker mason cut it to the correct size and shape on his bench and the banker with the fixer positioned it to the building. The banker mason carved a mark explaining where each stone was to be fixed and these can occasionally be seen on stones displaced from their position. Although no longer in operation, an interesting trip to see 2,000 years of quarrying is at Beer Quarry Caves in Devon **www.beerquarrycaves.co.uk**, where Beer stone, a form of chalk soft when mined but hard on exposure to air, has been quarried from underground caverns since Roman times. Because it is easy to carve and a wonderful creamy white colour when exposed to air, this stone was used in tracery work at Westminster Abbey, Windsor Castle and Hampton Court. Imagine the challenge of transporting four-ton blocks by cart or water from Devon to their final destination…

The Book of Trades explains that cutting larger stones was the stone cutter's job, although a mason often did it. It is also erroneously believed that a mason carved stone, but in reality it was the carver, although a mason occasionally took on simple carving work. A mason's tools included a square level, plumb line, bevel, compass, hammer, chisel, mallet and saw, which for masonry had no teeth; the weight of the saw cut through stone. For information on the types of marble, stone and mortars and working with it, refer to *The Book of Trades*.

Limestone is among the most common stone for building and carving and has several varieties: the Houses of Parliament are built in Anston from Yorkshire; York Minster is from magnesian limestone and St Paul's Cathedral is built from Dorset Portland stone. The incredible stone carving that embellishes so many of our cathedrals is witness to the skills of the stone carver working with nothing more than hand tools of hammer and chisel.

A journeyman stone mason received between four shillings and four shillings and sixpence a day, a good wage of just under £1 a week. In 1806, he charged for his work by the cubic foot, charging extra for iron clamps and cutting holes for railings. Piece work was common and a stone mason/carver working on an elaborate design expected to receive at least twice as much.

By 1865, bricklayers, masons, carpenters and smiths building the Albert Embankment in London earned six shillings and sixpence a day. Strikes reduced working hours from eleven and a half in the early 1860s to ten hours a day, six days a week by 1865. Perhaps highlighting the importance of brick and bricklayers versus stone, the number of masons decreased during the middle of Victoria's reign; in 1851, 101,442 men were recorded as masons/paviors, but by 1871 it was 95,243. A stone mason's apprenticeship traditionally lasted seven years.

Thatchers

The word thatch comes from old English *thac* meaning roof covering and was the most common form of roofing until the seventeenth century; if an old house has a roof pitched more than fifty degrees, it was probably previously thatched. Thatch was warm and cheap, but its major disadvantage was the fire risk and it was banned in

London as early as 1212. Hayricks were thatched after harvest to prevent rain ruining them and, although agricultural labourers were adept at this, specialised thatchers also did it. Some suggest the best local thatcher took Thatcher as a surname.

The type of straw depended on what was locally available. Until the arrival of the railways, enabling cheaper, easier and faster transportation, thatchers utilised local materials. The Midlands, Oxfordshire and the south of England used long wheat straw, whereas East Anglia used local water reed transported via its extensive waterways. This reed was prized because it grew to seven feet in length and, because it grew in water, was particularly hardwearing. In a year of a bad harvest, rye straw might be used. Less popular materials included rushes, sedge and heather. The style of thatching is localised, with different counties sporting different patterns. Straw as a harvest by-product had many other uses besides thatching: straw ropes, hats (see Chapter 9), mats, rush seats for chairs, corn dollies and stuffing horse collars.

After grain harvesting, straw for thatching was dried for two to three weeks in the fields as stooks. It was then bundled into *yealms* and attached to the roof with hazel spars – twisted and split hazel sticks 30 inches long. It was usual, and still is, for just the top of the roof to be repaired, so old houses have thatch several feet deep with the bottom layers perhaps over 500 years old. The edge of the thatched roof was cut and shaped using a long eaves knife. Other tools required for thatching include the leggat (a square flat tool imbedded with horse-shoe nails for bashing straw into position), a straw comb, shearing hooks and a spar knife.

Very often, a thatcher trained his sons in the craft; from 1727, the Marsters of Guilden Morden had several generations of thatchers. There was no thatchers' guild and the National Council of Master Thatchers Association (NCMTA founded 1987) suggests it was because communication was difficult for a trade spread so widely over the country. Current county thatching trade associations were formed as recently as 1947 from existing thatching families and are represented by the NCMTA.

The Museum of English Rural Life based at Reading University and its Scottish equivalent, the National Museum of Rural Life based in East Kilbride, might give you a feel for the life of a thatcher, blacksmith, cartwright and wheelwright. Many archives in the Museum of English Rural Life have been catalogued and are accessible via The National Archives Discovery website **http:// discovery.nationalarchives.gov.uk**. For thatchers, once references to Margaret Thatcher have been discounted, there are accounts relating to, inter alia, an unnamed thatcher's bills in 1795 Cornwall. The subsequent entry in Discovery was Turnor's (sic) Charity Account Book for Bedfordshire, where we learn the cost of the thatcher's materials in the late 1700s: the straw for thatching a barn in 1783 cost thirteen shillings, seven and a half pence, four bunches of thatching ropes one shilling and four pence; two bundles of thatching rods one shilling. In 1766, the thatcher must have completed a larger job because here he was paid £1 five shillings and ten pence.

Chapter 7
SMITHS AND METAL WORKERS

Gold is for the mistress – silver for the maid
Copper for the craftsman cunning at his trade.
'Good!' said the Baron, sitting in his hall,
'But Iron – Cold Iron – is master of them all.'
Rudyard Kipling, *Cold Iron*

The streets of London were, legend told us, paved with gold and the Industrial Revolution was based on the black arts – not of magic – but manufacturing. Before 1700, only twelve types of metal were known: gold, copper, silver, lead, tin, iron, mercury, arsenic, antimony, zinc, bismuth and platinum. By 1800, there were twenty-four.

Blacksmiths

See also wheelwrights (Chapter 10) and ironmongers (Chapter 5).

Joe Gargery and Pip (Dickens' *Great Expectations*) were blacksmiths (often shortened to smith). A blacksmith worked with 'black' metal – iron with its black oxide once finished – and there were so many that Smith is the most common surname in the English language. Labouring in dangerous conditions, they made and mended iron implements such as harrows, pokers, firedogs, shovels, tools like scythe blades and hammers, gates and fencing. Although the farrier was responsible for treating horse ailments as well as shoeing, smiths occasionally made horseshoes and constructed and fitted metal rims for wheelwrights. Every village of necessity had a smithy, often sited at a convenient crossroads. After the arrival of the horseless carriage, it was the village blacksmith who became a mechanic to change with the times.

Smith and wheelwright combined forces to make cartwheels. The area in front of the smithy was deliberately kept clear for this purpose. The trick was to make the metal tyre smaller than the wheel, heat it until the metal expanded to fit the wheel, hammer it into position and douse it with water before hot metal burnt wood. The metal tyre should fit the wheel snugly and perfectly.

The most important equipment in a smithy was the forge and its large chimney, anvil, block and bellows operated by the apprentice. Tools as detailed in *The Book of Trades* 1806 included the sledge hammer, smaller hammers, tongs, files, punches, chisels and pincers to hold and work with red and white hot metal. In front of the forge was the trough of water for rapidly cooling hot metal and wetting coals to make them burn hotter.

Early man used charcoal to smelt iron from iron ore. Coal may have been used when available but was an unsuitable fuel because sulphur reacted with the iron, causing it to crumble. The blacksmith called this 'hot or red short'. Charcoal making devoured trees so extensively that there was a serious shortage before the Industrial Revolution and research shows more trees in England today than 300 years ago.

In 1709, Quaker Abraham Derby (1678–1717) developed a process to turn cheap coal, not wood, into charcoal to make coke for blast furnaces. Consequently, the production of cast and wrought iron was considerably cheaper, could be made on a bigger scale and led directly to the Industrial Revolution. Coke was also a by-product of the gasworks; coal burnt in resorts produced gas and the resultant coke could be bought direct by any blacksmith or coal merchant living nearby. Blacksmiths today, when they can get it, still use high quality coke or gas. Abraham Derby's blast furnace can be visited at Coalbrookdale Museum of Iron.

There is more to smithing than merely beating hot metal with a hammer. The temperature of the iron was specific to each job and what was being produced. A smith had no thermometer and skilfully judged temperature according to the colour of the fire and the metal; iron became red, orange, yellow then white. Forging heat, the most useful, was yellow-orange. Iron melts at white hot. The hotter the fire, the softer the metal. For welding two pieces of metal together, the heat needs to be extremely high. The metal beating is crucial; the skill lies in where to strike the metal and how hard. Lighter strokes are required for more intricate work. Brittle cast iron could not be beaten with hammers. A smith's labourer and apprentice helped with hammering and turning metal and using the bellows. Without the smith, we wouldn't have those fabulous Georgian terraces, for it was the smith who made cast iron railings and fixed them to the house.

Smiths charged by the weight of items made. They might ask six pence per pound for railings and window bars. Ornamental work, because of its intricacy, was more expensive; brackets and lamp irons, for instance, would be between eight and fourteen pence per pound. Cast iron railings and sash weights were fifteen shillings to eighteen shillings per hundredweight. A journeyman smith received between three and five shillings a day, but a specialist in intricate work earned considerably more.

A fascinating insight into the life and temperament of Sherington blacksmith Bill Clark and his previous incumbent Bill Groom was published on page fifteen of the *Bucks Standard* on 27 December 1968. Blacksmiths were 'bluff, independent and kindly,' and in the author's opinion, 'craftmanship involved a balanced use of hand, brain and eye and the result was contentment'. The article describes a distinctive plough fashioned by Bill Clark and wheelwright Georgie Hyne, who made entire farm carts, not just wheels, and 'luxuriated' in the feel of wood under his hands.

My father tells me that when he was working in the early 1930s at boiler maker firm Daniel Adamsons, Dukinfield, blacksmiths wore white coats and were regarded more highly than any other workers. Daniel Adamsons' records for 1869–1984 are held at Cheshire Archives and Local Studies Centre in Chester.

A whitesmith worked with white metal such as tin or polished metalwork to a highly polished finish. Often known as tinners or tinsmiths, they mended pots and pans for the poor, many travelling the country with a backpack; the tinker. John Bunyan, author of *The Pilgrim's Progress*, called himself a tinker, walking the countryside preaching, but genealogists must be aware that some tinkers were vagrants with a poor reputation. Their raw material was tin plate, flat plates of iron covered in tin to prevent it rusting. A brightsmith generally worked cold metal. Under the generic term blacksmith, some artisans specialised in making bells or locks and keys.

The Worshipful Company of Blacksmiths **http://blacksmiths company.org** is fortieth in the order of precedence and its earliest records date from 1299. Its website has an excellent explanation of its history. Records and archives from the end of the fifteenth century to the present day include minutes, accounts and bindings of apprentices, the boys' fathers' names and their and town of origin. Many boys originated from outside London. Clocksmiths, gunsmiths, armourers and farriers might also belong, often at loggerheads with each other. Anchorsmiths from the Royal College of Deptford could also be members. Pre-1828 records are held in the LMA/Guildhall, but the website warns family historians that there are no records for blacksmiths working outside London.

From the middle of the eighteenth century, most blacksmiths worked outside Company control and records of working smiths were not kept. The best line of inquiry is apprenticeship records which, as legal documents, had to be registered. Most boys were apprenticed at fourteen for seven years. For boys apprenticed outside London, records are sparse, but try county museums and record offices for the area where your ancestor lived.

Durham's records held at the university include records for whitesmiths and blacksmiths, amongst others, for the eighteenth to twentieth centuries. Auctioneers Rowley Son and Royce sold the contents of Mr Richards's blacksmith shop, Wimpole, in October 1837, itemising out all the tools and valuing each of them. Examples include a grindstone and frame for ten shillings and a screw-spanner and four spike bits for two shillings and sixpence. The total valuation for the fifty items was £28 18s 6d.

Mr Richard's blacksmith shop, Wimpole. Sale inventory dated 10 October 1837 from Rowley Son and Royce auctioneers' records. (Courtesy Cambridgeshire Archives 296/B759)

The London Lives project **www.londonlives.org** gives a voice to 'plebeian' Londoners. Type 'blacksmith' in the search box and you will find a plethora of wills proven from 1680 and records of birth and biographies of felons executed at Newgate Prison. This includes Fulham-born fourteen-year-old blacksmith's apprentice Thomas Weal, who fell into bad company in 1685. Twenty-three year old Nathaniel Page, a farrier's apprentice in Fulham but originally from Somerset, stole several gold guineas for which, we read, he was vastly sorry. He was also in Newgate Prison in 1685.

Most blacksmith trade union information in the Modern Records Centre **www2.warwick.ac.uk/services/library/mrc** is twentieth century, although there are registration books and financial reports dating from 1857, some mentioning names of deceased members and their wives. Unfortunately, they are not indexed and you must wade through year by year to find any information. Go to the 'Looking for an Ancestor?' section.

The Working Class Movement Library in Salford **www.wcml.org. uk** has quarterly and annual reports, mainly from 1920, as well as some obituaries and grants for blacksmiths belonging to the Associated Blacksmiths, Forge and Smithy Workers Society.

The Shropshire Record Office has the Company of Smiths minute and apprentice book for 1622–1764 (ref 6001/4583) and it is worth checking other local record offices for your blacksmith, especially as this precedes the volunteer-compiled Blacksmith Index.

The volunteer-created Blacksmith Index **http://blacksmiths. mygenwebs.com** includes all blacksmiths appearing in censuses, plus any further information the compilers may have found. Compiled county by county, it has a surname index redirecting you to the county and page of the specified person. Related trades such as locksmith, anchorsmith and goldsmiths are included, as well as some social history anecdotes under 'interesting stories'.

The Worshipful Company of Farriers **www.wcf.org.uk** was established as a fellowship in London in 1356 but, like many London guilds, lost its early records in the Great Fire. Its charter, reproduced online, was received in 1674. Of more interest to the family historian is a basic qualification introduced in 1887, the Registered Shoeing Smith (RSS) and an examination system from 1890. From 1923, farriers had to pass a difficult examination which, if successful, gave the title Fellow of the Worshipful Company of Farriers, FWCF. Unfortunately, many records were lost in the Blitz, but surviving records can be viewed at Guildhall Library and include lists of apprentices, details of examination passes, freemen and Liverymen (who may not be registered farriers) from 1610 onwards.

Local newspapers are a mine of information for any family

historian and, once you have the location of your craftsman, check the local papers either at the relevant records office or library or at the British Library newspaper collection. Many local libraries are indexing records and newspapers and you may find an article describing an ancestor of yours. The British Newspaper Archive **www.britishnewspaperarchive.co.uk** is a subscription service.

There are working forges around the country. Although it is not possible to visit commercial enterprises, several open-air museums, St Fagans National History Museum in Cardiff **www.museum wales.ac.uk/stfagans**, Chiltern Open Air Museum **www.coam. org.uk** and Avoncroft Museum, Bromsgrove **www.avoncroft.org.uk** have forges, some running short blacksmith courses.

Goldsmiths and Silversmiths

Assaying and marking gold with the King's mark has been the responsibility of the Goldsmiths' Company **www.thegoldsmiths. co.uk** since at least 1300. The Goldsmiths received their first Royal Charter in 1327, although there is evidence of a guild in London as early as 1179. Its London assay mark, a leopard's head, wore a crown until 1822. Gold and silver is also hallmarked in Birmingham, Edinburgh and Sheffield.

By the fifteenth century, the Assay Office hallmarked, with the mark of the Hall, gold and silver artefacts made by London craftsmen. No one was immune to charges of fraud, so not only did it assay gold but, from the twelfth century, it also periodically checked that the Royal Mint's coins were the right weight and metal composition. This *Trial of the Pyx* still takes place annually, with the Master of the Mint, the current Chancellor of the Exchequer, 'on trial'. The Latin word '*pyx*' means a chest and the coins were originally stored in large chests in the Pyx Chamber in Westminster Abbey.

Goldsmiths made artefacts, jewellery, plates, bowls and church regalia from precious metal. Because gold, especially higher carats, is very malleable, this required less force than iron. Like a blacksmith, they poured molten metal into moulds using the lost wax method and engraved, filed, turned and polished their products. These were often jobs in their own right but only the master's mark was stamped on the article. An apprenticeship lasted up to ten years depending on the craft and an illiterate apprentice might have an extra two years added to his indenture to teach him to read. It is important to remember that someone apprenticed in London could later work anywhere in the country, as shown in the records.

In 1851, there were 11,242 gold and silversmiths recorded in the census; by 1871, this had doubled to 22,031. For a contemporary 1860s view of the Bank of England, gold coins and bank notes, see pages 526 to 544 of Daniel Joseph Kirwan's *Palace and Hovel*, published 1870 **https://archive.org/stream/palacehovel00kirw# page/526/mode/2up**.

The Goldsmiths were well-known for philanthropy. Under the terms of his will, Sir Edmund Shaa, Lord Mayor of London 1482–83 and Master of the Royal Mint, founded Stockport Grammar School, still in existence. Alderman John Perryn (will dated 1656) bequeathed money and land on which almshouses were built in Acton, West London. Although sold in 2000, they can still be seen on Churchfield Road and some neighbouring streets such as Shaa Road have goldsmith-related names. Records for people benefitting from them, if in existence, are difficult to find.

The London Goldsmiths' apprentice records dating from 1578 are held at the Goldsmiths' Company Library on the first floor of its Hall in Foster Lane, London. They list the name of the apprentice, parent and if they were living or dead, the parent's trade and parish where they lived. If the apprentice became a freeman, their name is recorded in the freedom books dating from 1692. Before this, names were written in the Court Minute Books from 1334. These also hold references to goldsmiths, not necessarily members of the Company, falling foul of the ordinances (rules). You might find the mark of your ancestor in the Goldsmiths' records, which include their address and date of the issued maker's mark, but unfortunately two eighteenth-century registers are missing. However, you might find your London goldsmith ancestor in *London Goldsmiths, 1697–1837: Their Marks and Lives from the Original Registers at Goldsmiths Hall and Other Sources* by Arthur Grimwade. This book includes goldsmiths, bankers and pawnbrokers and addresses for goldsmiths and their shops in London. *Chester Goldsmiths from Early Times to 1726*, by Maurice Hill Ridgeway, is helpful for Chester ancestors. The Rollco project is a free search engine at **www.londonroll.org** and includes records for several London livery companies. The Goldsmiths' records of apprentices cover, at the time of writing, 1600–1700 with ambitions to expand it from 1575 to the mid-twentieth century, although the timescale for this is unclear.

For further information about London goldsmith ancestors, try contacting the Librarian at Goldsmiths' Hall by email or post, with the full name and dates of your ancestor and any further information such as their address. The library is open by appointment from 10am to 4.45pm Monday to Friday so telephone 020 7606 7010 or email **library@thegoldsmiths.co.uk**. To help, they need as much *relevant* information as possible beforehand. Please do not send extended accounts of the family's genealogy. What is held on their archives can be found on **www.aim25.ac.uk** and search for Goldsmiths' Company and Goldsmiths' Library. A brief account of the Company history is on the website.

Shropshire Record Office holds admissions and apprentice rolls for goldsmiths from 1424–1838 (ref 6001/4257-4270), Durham City Guilds records, held at the university, have Goldsmith records from the seventeenth to twentieth century. Check the relevant record office for your ancestors.

Jewellers and Watch/Clockmakers

Adorning and decorating the body is nothing new. In the Bible, Aaron had a breast plate studded with precious jewels; and necklaces and bracelets were found in Egyptian pyramids. This craft is often interchangeable with that of the goldsmith. A visit to any museum, especially the British Museum, parades their skill in all its splendour.

Jacob Winter pub sign over a former jewellery shop in Stockport town centre, showing a jeweller at work. (©Adèle Emm)

Caleb Masters, journeyman baker 1851, master baker 1861. The chain for his half-hunter watch, made by Coales and Sons, can clearly be seen. (Author's collection, ©Adèle Emm)

The Book of Trades' definition of a jeweller is someone who sets precious stones into gold, but who also makes rings, lockets, bracelets, necklaces, earrings etc. It admires 'English jewellers, for excellence of workmanship, have been and still are, superior to every other nation', explaining the cutting and grinding of diamonds, pearls and their quality, type of tools and equipment and how a workshop must be kept warm as jewellers cannot work in the cold. A forge for fashioning the precious metal is required, as is, of course, a workbench and lathe. In 1806, the jewellery trade was largely based in London but the American War of Independence (1775–83) reduced many to penury. The top rate of pay for a journeyman was four guineas a week, but more realistic payment was twenty-eight to thirty-nine shillings.

On his deathbed, my great-grandfather auctioned off his half-hunter watch (don't ask), which was bought by my grandfather. Made in Newport Pagnell in the middle of the nineteenth century by jeweller/watchmaker Coales and Sons, this was my grandfather's prize possession. Coales, in business from at least the 1830s, are well recorded throughout censuses, newspapers, directories, electoral and parish registers and wills. They are respectively described as jewellers, watchmaker jeweller, silversmiths and gold jeweller and held other interests besides the shop; one family member was a printer and stationer in 1871 and a wife and daughter ran a ladies' school in 1891, her husband now a private resident. Intriguingly, in 1851 jeweller Harry Goldstint, described as a 'Prussian Jew,' lodged with an innkeeper in the High Street. The number of watch and clockmakers recorded in the censuses remained virtually the same between 1851 (19,159) and 1871, with a mere 2,000 more.

Of course, not all jewellers made watches and not all clock and watchmakers made jewellery. Within a shop, it was common for one person to make and repair clocks and watches whilst another specialised in jewellery. Not only did a jeweller/watchmaker make watches and clocks, but they often made the tools and individual parts. Watchmaking tools and procedures are explained on **www.csparks.com/watchmaking**.

Half-hunter watch and chain made by Coales and Sons of Newport Pagnell: their signature is inscribed on the watch. (©Adèle Emm)

Up until the introduction of the railways, when timetables required trains to be punctual and clocks to be accurate, it didn't matter if the church clock was out of kilter with the neighbouring village. In rural areas, people rose and went to bed by the sun. The first clock to be installed on a church was Salisbury Cathedral in 1386, followed by Wells Cathedral six years later; the mechanism is in the Science Museum. Those wealthy enough in England to afford a timepiece in the late sixteenth century obtained one from Germany or the Low Countries, especially when religious persecution meant immigrants crossed the Channel to make clocks and watches in London. Calvinist Geneva in 1556 charged its goldsmiths with idolatry and, as they were prevented from making jewellery, they turned their hand to watches instead. English clockmakers with backgrounds in locksmithing, blacksmithing and needlemaking made their way from the provinces to London, but by the seventeenth century rivalry from immigrant craftsmen (no change there) meant the Blacksmiths' Guild in particular felt threatened. It wasn't until 1631 that a breakaway group gained a Royal Charter from Charles I for a Clockmakers' Guild. The start of the Civil War eleven years later put paid to the guild for the duration. Like locksmiths, blacksmiths and needlemakers, jewellers had the necessary skill for such fiddly, meticulous work.

Claudius Saunier, in his fascinating 1881 *Watchmaker's Handbook* **https://archive.org/stream/watchmakershand00tripgoog** warns the watchmaker about associated health issues. Close work and the constant use of a strong lens could result in conjunctivitis which, pre-antibiotics, could lead to blindness. He recommends a green cardboard lampshade to protect the eyes from radiation and warns of 'the dazzling light of gas' suggesting that bathing eyes with cold water and staring at large stationary objects will help. For him, short-sighted boys should not be apprenticed because eyesight deteriorates under the strain of detailed work, but he contradictorily cites an opthalmist (sic) who claims close work *preserves* the eyesight! Sensibly, considering a jeweller needs a steady hand, he warns against alcohol and tobacco use. Like a modern-day health and safety manual, he recommends the correct bench height, cautioning that middle-aged watchmakers are bad tempered due to poor posture. Aside from his warnings, we now know mercury used in barometers and pendulums had its own perils (see hat making, Chapter 9) and high temperatures when smelting metals and the use of acid can result in bad burns.

A useful book – the SoG has a copy – is *Britten's Old Clocks and Watches and their Makers*, originally published in 1894 and reissued by Methuen in 1982. This lists, in alphabetical order, all watch and clockmakers, dates and towns where they worked itemising famous watches. There is little biographical information, but it shows what an ancestor produced. Some researchers and archivists have indexed clock and watchmakers for various counties and the SoG and local record offices may hold copies. Edward Legg (1937–2008) compiled one for Buckinghamshire **www.dumville.org/stories/clockmakers _b1.html**. A partial list of Northampton clockmakers compiled by W.N. Terry, curator of Northampton Museum and Art Gallery, is online at **www.edintone.com/watchmakers**. Ann Spiro has assembled **http://freepages.genealogy.rootsweb.ancestry.com/~ blacksmiths/clockmakers-1.htm**. Ancestry, in its occupations section, has G.H. Baillie's 1947 *Watchmakers and Clockmakers of the World* online. The Company of Clockmakers **www.clockmakers.org** has helpful information and a booklist.

Many early clocks and watches made in London are housed in the oldest clock collection in the world. Providing a fascinating history and explanation of how watches and clocks were made, the Clockmakers' Museum, established 1814, is moving after a 140-year sojourn at Guildhall to London's Science Museum, opening summer 2015. Other clock and watch exhibitions include those at the V & A, Science Museum, British Museum and the Royal Observatory at Greenwich. Outside London, amongst others, are: Hollytrees Museum, Colchester; the Dorset Collection of Clocks in Dorchester; Belmont Clocks at Faversham, Kent; the Clock Trust, Funtington, West Sussex and the Usher Gallery, Lincoln, which houses the collection of jeweller and watchmaker James Usher (1845–1921). For museums and collections around the world, try **www.nawcc-index.net/Museums.php**.

Locksmiths

To protect their possessions, the Ancient Egyptians made locks from wood. From Roman times, locks and keys were metal and, although bulky, could be carried on the person. Unfortunately for the owner, if not the thief, keys were virtually the same design with a cylindrical shaft and single tooth. The modern flat key with pins was invented as late as the mid-1800s by Linus Yale, and was unavailable in the UK until 1911 at the earliest. From 1818, following a competition to find a lock which couldn't be broken, the winner Jeremiah Chubb produced in his Wolverhampton factory high-quality locks which thwarted picking. The name is still famous today. The Chubb Collectanea in the LMA, although it has minimal genealogical information, may be of interest to anyone whose ancestors worked in the locksmith trade (or were burglars) **www.cityoflondon. gov.uk/things-to-do**.

A locksmith made locks, keys, padlocks and safes. Interestingly, Abraham Derby of coke fame (see Blacksmiths) was the son of a yeoman farmer and locksmith. The principal centres were Willenhall, Staffordshire, where Yale is still based, and neighbouring Wolverhampton; locks were made in both towns from the sixteenth century. Lockmaking is listed as the principal trade of the seventeenth century in Wolverhampton and trade directories from the late seventeenth century list many of the lockmakers in town. Red Book Directories might be useful and copies are held in Wolverhampton Archives and Local Studies.

Pigot's Directory for Willenhall for 1834 lists and names fifteen bolt makers, two brassfounders and casters, three dye sinkers, five file makers, five iron and steel warehouses, ninety key makers, eleven key stampers, 280 lock makers and seventeen spring latch makers as well as two spur makers for South America! A brief glimpse at virtually every page of the 1851 census shows a locksmith family neighbouring another, with twelve-year-old boys citing it as their occupation. By 1855, there were 340 locksmiths in the area, employing their entire family in a backyard workshop where children filed keys and hours were a brutal 6am to 7pm. A locksmith apprentice working up to eighteen hours a day slumped over a bench might develop a hump-back and crooked left leg, leading to Willenhall's nickname of 'Humpshire'. According to the Children's Employment Commission report of 1843, they might be 'cruelly beaten' with a stick, hammer handle or 'whatever came to hand'. If work wasn't sold this week, there was no money to buy raw materials for next week.

Why Willenhall? Because, like Stockport in Cheshire where hat makers were paid less than those in London, Willenhall locksmiths earned less than locksmiths in Wolverhampton, who made more complicated, higher quality and therefore more expensive locks. Those made in Willenhall might cost a penny each, and were exported all over the world because they were so cheap. By 1860, like the hatting and shoemaking industries, locks were produced in factories rather than backyard workshops. The workforce was largely female and far cheaper than men.

Like so many working-class trades, it is difficult to find genealogical details for locksmiths other than census records. Online forums request help with hard-to-find relatives which may offer a solution. A website giving information about keys and lock making is found at **www.historyofkeys.com/locks-history/history-of-locksmithing** and Willenhall and Wolverhampton websites are useful for background to the area. As always, try local record offices.

An interesting visit for anyone with a locksmith in their family history is the Black Country Living Museum's Locksmith's House **www.bclm.co.uk/locations/the-locksmiths-house** in Willenhall, where locksmith Richard Hodson plied his trade from 1792. The family, working in a two-storey workhouse behind their house, specialised in bar padlocks. The house later became a drapery. The museum holds demonstrations of lock making and there is a working forge and lock gallery. Visits must be booked in advance.

Chapter 8
CORDWAINERS AND SHOEMAKERS

Brave shoemakers, all gentlemen of the gentle craft.
Thomas Dekker (1572?–1632)

Shoes and shoemaking are so integral to life that it is the stuff of myth and legend. To ward off evil spirits, an old shoe was hidden in a building when it was built or renovated. In one fairy tale, elves help a shoemaker make his fortune; leprechauns make one shoe for fairies, never a pair. Shoemaker Hans Christian Anderson was more successful at writing fairy stories than shoemaking and some suggest Cinderella's glass slipper was a mistranslation from French *vers* (fur) for *verre* (glass). An old woman lived in a shoe in one nursery rhyme and in another:

Cobbler cobbler mend my shoe,
Get it done by half past two.
Stitch it up and stitch it down,
Then I'll walk around the town.

As one of the oldest forms of clothing, shoes have protected our feet from rocks, stones and thistles since we were cavemen. In 2010, preserved by a plentiful supply of sheep dung much like our own Lindow Pete, a 5,500-year-old soft leather shoe, similar to a moccasin and stuffed with grass, was found in an Armenian cave. Soldiers in the Crimean War (1853–56) would appreciate this; when they removed their boots after battle, they filled them with dry grass to reduce the sweat (and presumably the smell) before replacing them next day. There are suggestions that the lack of grass in the First World War was a contributory factor to trench foot.

The patron saints of shoemakers are Saint Crispin and his brother Saint Crispinian who, when preaching in Gaul and Britain, supported themselves by making shoes. It is because of them that shoemaking is 'the gentle craft'. When Thomas Dekker wrote the line above, shoemakers considered themselves a cut above other trades and were masters of their own working practices and hours. All changed under the factory system.

At a Saxon marriage, the father delivered his daughter's shoe to the groom, who tapped his bride's forehead with it during the ceremony to show his authority. One of the earliest craftsmen to land in America was shoemaker Christopher Nelme, who sailed from Bristol to Virginia in 1619.

Most of us have shoe and bootmakers, cordwainers, binders and such like in our family tree – not surprising when virtually every village had a shoemaker who occasionally doubled as cobbler, refitting shoes for other wearers if he were short of work.

In 1851, 274,451 people were employed in boot and shoemaking, the fourth largest employment behind farming and farm workers, servants and the textile industries.

Certain towns were 'shoe towns'; Northampton's football team is nicknamed 'The Cobblers'. Clarks made shoes in Street, Somerset, until manufacture moved abroad at the end of the twentieth century. Staffordshire and Norwich had a thriving shoe industry and a history of Leicester's shoemaking industry is found on **www.british-history.ac.uk/report.aspx?compid=66568**. Dr Martens (the Griggs family worked in Northampton from 1901, buying German brand Dr Martens in 1960) are now largely made in China, although the Vintage brand is still made in Wollaston, Northamptonshire. Manufactured in Skelmersdale, Hotter buck the trend. Once famous chain stores, Barratts, and Freeman, Hardy and Willis have left the high street and Timpsons cuts keys and repairs shoes when once it made them. In shoe towns, it was common to find entire streets where everyone, including daughters, worked in the shoe industry. This also occurred in towns not specifically associated with shoemaking; London's East End, Hackney, Bethnal Green and

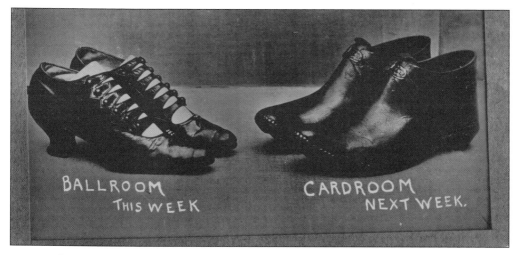

Postcard showing the skill and care taken in making Edwardian shoes. (Author's collection, ©Adèle Emm)

Shoreditch for example. A statue of a cordwainer is found in the cordwainer quarter established in 1104 near Cheapside in the City of London **www.cordwainer.co.uk**; *Cheap* meant market in medieval English. In Saxon, *Cepa* meant merchant and *ceapian* to buy.

So what is the difference between cordwainers, shoe makers, snobs and cobblers? Shoemakers made shoes and bootmakers boots, usually for military wear. Cordwainers were leather workers. *Cordwain* is a corruption of 'cordovan', a soft leather from Cordoba, Spain and effectively, cordwainers made expensive, better shoes but, because they worked in leather, could turn their hand to saddles, harnesses (see Chapter 10), gloves (see Chapter 9), travelling cases and bags. Cordwaining was the superior craft, but a man might categorise himself as cordwainer in one census and shoemaker in the following.

As defined by the Oxford English Dictionary, the origin of the word 'snob' is obscure, but is a colloquial dialect term for a cobbler first recorded in 1781. One suggestion is that a cobbler, a snob, was the epitome of bad breeding, hence the modern understanding of the word. Cobblers reconditioned boots and shoes. In 1861, when a pair of working boots could cost fifteen shillings, many only owned one pair, making it imperative to keep them in good order. In Daniel Kirwan's 1860s description of London in *Palace and Hovel* (p394) he writes that 2,500 men patched and mended shoes, earning four to seven shillings a week, or ten shillings in a good week.

Before a leather worker made shoes, he must buy the leather. The tanner tanned it and the currier prepared the leather for the saddler or shoemaker. For further historical information about this process, see *The Book of Trades*, 1806. A major market for prepared leather in the early nineteenth century was London's Leadenhall Market, to where shoemakers and other leather workers travelled for their hides. The Company of Curriers **www.curriers.co.uk**, twenty-ninth in the order of precedence, received its ordinances in 1415. In 1590, although the Company of Curriers had always by necessity had a close relationship with the Company of Cordwainers, a law was passed to prevent contention between the two, ensuring all leather was brought to Leadenhall and Southwark markets and cured and dressed within three miles of London. Outside London, leather workers obtained their leather from local tanners and curriers.

A shoemaker or cordwainer served an apprenticeship. Working tools included a shoemaker's bench and selection of tools, often combined; awls, lasting pincers, knives, hammer, augurs, files and rasps. Most worked in a workshop at home, often on their own, whilst others employed an apprentice or time-served journeyman. He might employ his daughter as binder, the process at the end of shoe making when shoes were waterproofed by adding wax (binder) to the gap between sole, upper and heel. He frequently employed his wife to close the uppers and in shoe factories today women still close the uppers. Commonly, a tanner, shoemaker and saddler inhabited the same house, working the same leather. In Bethnal Green, several generations of shoemakers, alongside other trades, lived in Minerva Street just off Hackney Road. Walter Thomas Emm lived here in the 1830s with his father and an eleven-year-old apprentice. His brother remained in the same street until 1911. Although the area has been extensively redeveloped, handbag shops still trade in Hackney Road.

It was not a lucrative craft. Shoemakers went bankrupt (reported in *London Gazette*). Others lived hand-to-mouth, supplementing their shoemaking income by other means. Walter Thomas Emm, who alternated between calling himself cordwainer and shoemaker, occasionally collected rents for widow Mary Emsley of Whitechapel and was accused alongside plasterer James Mullins of her brutal murder in August 1860. From the discovery of the body until the end of the trial in October, this infamous murder was reported daily in *The Times* and as far as the *Cornwall Chronicle* and *New York Evening Express*.

Throughout the trial transcripts, we glimpse the life of a Victorian cordwainer/shoemaker. Walter's family lived in a cottage with a shed to one side, probably his workshop, on wasteland behind Mrs Emsley's house. Not only was this area insalubrious 'an open field; persons have no right there, but they can get in very easily – the palings appear to be knocked down,' but there was a ruined cottage in the same field. Mullins diverted attention from himself by accusing Emms (sic) of 'pretending to pick herbs' here. Walter lived with his wife and four children (one child had died beforehand); a total of six when chronic overcrowding was common. Incriminating evidence at the trial included shoemaking tools; 'a piece of tape which might form an apron string… a piece of shoemaker's waxed string'. Later, 'it is waxed with cobbler's wax'. And finally, 'Emm is by trade a shoemaker – I found his tools in his house; …I believe a shoemaker's hammer was amongst them.'

Walter was acquitted but Mullins was hanged. At his execution, Mullins' final speech was printed in the *Bucks Standard*, among others. Forty years later, Sir Arthur Conan Doyle revisited the case, confirming Emm's innocence and Mullins' guilt.

Bootmakers

In one census, a man might describe himself as a shoemaker and the subsequent one a bootmaker depending on what he was doing at the time. Boots were generally for military use. In the late 1780s, under the threat and ultimate declaration of war with France against Napoleon, they were made and stockpiled in a Northampton warehouse. From 1793, Leicester was also making standardised boots for the army; by 1810, the army needed boots for around 250,000 men. Another drive centred around the Crimean War in the 1850s which might explain why a man recorded himself as bootmaker in one census and shoemaker in another.

Military boots were made, as now, from very strong leather. Covered with dubbin to make them water resistant, this prevented boots from breathing, hence the practice of stuffing them with grass when not worn. Hobnails were for durability.

Boots were generally made in factories, although many bootmakers worked from home as outworkers. A factory could be a few men working together in a building or a large firm employing over 100 people.

Shoe Factories

Up until the mechanisation of the shoe industry, shoes were produced by traditional hand sewing and 'factories' from the 1760s were warehouses or central shops where shoes were put out to homeworkers. It was the invention of the sewing machine in the 1850s (see Chapter 9) that had massive repercussions on boot and shoe manufacture. In 1855 Singer marketed machines for the 'closing' element of shoe production i.e. when cut-out leather is stitched together to form the shoe upper. Fearing mechanisation and job loss, shoemakers in Northampton went on strike from March to July 1859.

American Lyman Reed Blake (1835–83) invented the eponymous Blake sole sewer which, by 1861, could stitch through upper and sole. By the 1860s, riveting machinery was used in boot making. Eventually various types of machinery, all with different functions, were housed together for convenience – the shoe factory. These consisted of several floors in a building, usually organised so that leather came in at the ground floor where the machinery was housed and shoes were finished and packed on the top floor.

Factories were in their heyday from the 1850s onwards until relocation abroad, for example to China, in the twentieth century. They had their own jargon for jobs with apprenticeships for many of them. These terms are found in census records, especially in shoe towns like Northampton or Stafford. The rough stuff worker and foreman cut ½ inch heavy leather hide and shaped it. The clicker was the 'elite', cutting out the upper part of the shoe and making the most of the leather by not wasting it, ensuring the grain matched in a pair of shoes – a pair of shoes was cut from the same hide. The 'click' came at the end of the process, the noise when the knife hit the wooden cutting board. The closer (always a woman and still is today) worked on a sewing machine joining the upper. Jobs in the closers' room included skiving, beading and lining and making eyelet holes for laces. There might be thirty operations in the closer's job. The laster was the operative joining soles to the upper and heel. A laster not working in a shoe factory made lasts or shoes from a last. A riveter hob-nailed sole to shoe. The finisher, located in the finishing room, usually on the top floor of the factory, trimmed, smoothed, coloured and glossed (polished) the shoes and put them into boxes. Finishing and closing was often done at home by outworkers who collected work from the factory and completed it in a room or outhouse converted to a workshop. Machinery could be hired from the factory. Paid by piecework, outworkers lost bonuses if quotas weren't completed. They were paid when they returned completed work to the factory.

Shoemaking factories had rules and regulations and, like many in the factory system, such as millworkers, pay was docked for tardiness. Generally, they couldn't visit other departments, were not permitted to smoke, send out for beer (!), swear or throw leather around the factory; **www.mylearning.org/victorian-shoemakers-in-northampton-1/images/1-4378**. Unions were permitted.

COPYRIGHT.

No 4. To think tha's to come back to these.

Comedy postcard from family album dated 1907, showing the irons and stitching in clogs. (Author's collection, ©Adèle Emm)

Clogmakers

Clogs were the footwear of farmers, rural workers, brewery workers and, of course, millworkers. The more expensive were carved to fit the wearer's foot. Hardwearing, they were made from wood which doesn't splinter e.g. birch, alder or sycamore and, for better durability, hobnails or irons shaped like horseshoes were fitted to the sole, the sound of which echoed on cobblestones in industrial northern cities. The leather uppers were nailed to the wooden sole.

After the Industrial Revolution, clog making and wearing was largely regional, confined to Wales and mill towns in Lancashire and Yorkshire. It waned after the First World War apart from mill towns. There were revivals during the Second World War; clogs weren't rationed so no coupons were required. During both world wars, when rubber for soles was required for the war effort, munition workers wore clogs without irons to prevent potentially fatal sparks. There was a brief hippy revival in the 1960s with Dr Scholls.

At the time of writing, there are only two traditional cloggers left in England making clogs entirely by hand; Walkely Clogs in Mytholmroyd, Yorkshire and Jeremy Atkinson in Herefordshire. Clog making demonstrations are occasionally held at Blists Hill, Ironbridge and Jeremy Atkinson occasionally does craft shows. See **www.clogmaker.co.uk**.

A job associated with clog making was the clog blocker who, working in gangs, chopped wood into rough sizes for children's, men's and women's feet.

There are several reasons for the demise of clogmakers. Fashion, the preference for hobnailed boots instead of clogs and the rise of machine-made clog soles.

Unions

The earliest trade unions were founded in the early 1800s and there were lots of them. Many were localised, such as the Edinburgh Operative Cordwainers Trade Protection and Friendly Society (1822) and records for 1912–56 are in the National Archives. There were specific unions such as the Amalgamated Journeyman Cloggers and Allied Workers (founded 1830) which, in Oldham in 1911, had 739 members. Bolton had its own cloggers union in existence in 1831. A useful directory for these unions is John B. Smethurst and Peter Carter's *Historical Directory of Trade Unions Volume Six* found on the internet under a hugely long URL but located with a Google search. Many unions amalgamated into the National Union of Boot and Shoe Operatives (1898) and the records including 1850-70s branch union books are held in the Warwick University Modern Record Centre. The union branch was known by the factory name so if someone moved jobs within the town, you will know by the change in their branch name. Other records, where they survive, are found in local record offices.

Records

The London Company of Cordwainers' records are held at Guildhall and can be searched on microfilm for free. The main genealogical information they hold is the Freedom records (1678 to present) and the Apprenticeship records from 1709 to 1965. They will do research for you for a fee of £20 plus VAT per name, but can't guarantee success.

In the 1870s, the Cordwainers and Leathersellers Companies set up a Cordwainers' College teaching footwear and leather trades to young people. The archives, consisting of a shoe collection, some journals, records and photographs of the College are held at the London College of Fashion and the shoe collection, many too fragile to exhibit, together with ephemera such as tools and lasts can be seen online at **www.vads.ac.uk/collections/LCFSHOE.html**.

There were other guilds throughout the country e.g. York and Cardiff, with records held locally. York Cordwainers Guild **http://yorkcordwainers.webplus.net/index.html** exists today as a philanthropic society and to promote the footwear and leather industries. The medieval guild disbanded in 1808 and its records were sent to the York Minster **www.yorkminster.org** where collections include ordinances for 1580–1694, 1580–1694 (with some signatures) for tanners, curriers, cordwainers and shoemakers. You will need a reader's ticket and an appointment. Durham Cordwainers' Guild and Curriers' records for the sixteenth to twentieth centuries are at the university, which also holds records for the seventeenth century for tanners and barkers who tanned leather using the bark of trees.

For Cardiff and Wales, *British History Online*, edited by John Hobson Matthews, itemises records for cordwainers and glovers including lists of members and their dates **http://www.british-history.ac.uk/source.aspx?pubid=375**. This website also lists company proceedings from 1676–1801, with names and other documents.

Northampton Museum and Art Gallery's shoe and boot collection and shoemakers' index, part on database and part on index cards, is one of the foremost collections in the world. Contact the museum with the relevant name and date and the museum can check them against the index. The museum is a mine of information on the history of major manufacturing companies, mainly in Northampton but also around the country. Northampton Museum and Art Gallery has a file containing books and articles on clog making and cloggers, but records for clogmakers are few, although apprentice records may be in local record offices. The museum sends business papers to the relevant local record office and you should check there. The museum has photos, trade catalogues for countrywide companies, a display of 1,000 shoes and a collection of over 13,000 shoes from around the world dating from Egyptian footwear to today; they actively encourage people to donate shoes. They also have runs of *Shoe and Leather Record*, *Shoe and Leather News*, *Boot and Shoe Trade Journals* and *St Crispin*. For further information, contact the museum via **www.northampton.gov.uk/museumcollections**.

The periodical *Shoe and Leather News* was published weekly from April 1916. It is an amazing record of the shoe industry, with adverts encompassing the whole industry as well as biographical information and articles about factories and owners/proprietors. Many adverts have photographs; for instance, Pollard and Son, Northampton, founded 1857 has three generations, the founder, E. Pollard, his son and grandson who joined the firm in 1900. The gazette element of the magazine includes, among other things, commercial and financial information around the country, bankruptcies and bills of sale, tribunals (not everyone is named), wills, obituaries, court cases and bankruptcies. Some wills include biographical information including hobbies and cause of death. Be prepared for a long hike through the magazines; they are not indexed so knowing dates is crucial. Finding someone is a bonus.

Bata's records **www.batamemories.org.uk** are held near the factory site at Bata Reminiscence and Resource Centre, East Tilbury Library, Princess Avenue, East Tilbury, Essex, RM18 8ST **www.thurrock.gov.uk/find-a-library/east-tilbury-library**. There is a small exhibition and regular open days are advertised online. Records can be visited by appointment; Bata volunteers are available at the library (01375 844921) Tuesdays, Thursdays and Saturday mornings at the time of writing. There is an extensive website including an index to former employees and short articles about some of them.

It may be worth checking the British Book Trade Index **www.bbti.bham.ac.uk**. Many tanners, curriers and fellmongers (hide and skin dealers) also worked peripherally in the parchment and paper making industries. This index has references to tradesmen years prior to the first useful census of 1841 and typing in a surname or name of a town might foster results. Newport Pagnell, for instance, brings up William Davis (it's harder to find specific ancestry records for a common surname) working as apprentice leather dresser/currier in 1716 and the source was the SoG's lists of masters and apprentices. His master was William Ward.

Places to visit – see also Chapter 9

• Jeremy Atkinson, clog maker, occasionally does craft shows. See his website for details at **www.clogmaker.co.uk**
• Northampton Museum and Art Gallery (shoe and boot collection), Northampton, **www.northampton.gov.uk/info/200243/museums** St Fagans National History Museum, Cardiff where Geraint Parfitt hand-makes clogs **www.museumwales.ac.uk/stfagans**
• Shoe Museum, Street, Somerset **www.streettic.co.uk/index. php?q=Shoe-Museum.html**
• Ward of Cordwainer **www.cordwainer.co.uk/content.php?id=67** information about the London ward including the Cordwainer statue (2002), Watling Street, London.

Chapter 9
CLOTHING AND ALLIED TRADES

With fingers weary and worn,
With eyelids heavy and red,
A woman sat, in unwomanly rags,
Plying her needle and thread –
Stitch! Stitch! Stitch!
In poverty, hunger and dirt,
And still with a voice of dolorous pitch
She sang 'The Song of the Shirt.'
Thomas Hood (1799–1845)

In the 1851 census, behind agricultural labourers and servants, the third most frequent occupation was cotton manufacturing, with over half a million people. Milliners/dressmakers were seventh. Add tailors and nearly a million people worked in the clothing trade, excluding shoemakers and hatting, out of a total population in England and Wales of 18 million people. Because of their low status, records are sparse and generally involve a trip to the record office.

The first mass-produced clothing is generally accepted as military uniforms for the 1812 war with France. However, for those unable to afford a dressmaker or tailor, ready-to-wear clothes were bought from 'slopshops', or sweat shops making and selling clothes; Pepys mentions a slop seller called Burrows in his diary entry for 21 March 1665. If you couldn't afford this, acquiring second-hand (third/fourth-hand) clothing elsewhere was your only option.

Writing in 1850, Henry Mayhew (1812–87), co-founder of *Punch*, describes a London sweat shop in disturbing terms. Seven workmen sitting cross-legged on the floor worked in a room about eight feet square, surrounded by sleeve boards, irons and material, making coats, jackets, vests, cloaks and trousers for slopshops, for which they received between five shillings and six pence and six shillings and nine pence for a frock coat taking two and a half days to make. Trimmings and thread were bought from their pay and four shillings a week was deducted to pay the master for food, tea and bed. One tailor commented that his working week was sixteen hours a day, seven days a week for thirteen shillings, for which, after deductions, he received seven shillings and three pence, adding that wages were higher in 1847.

Tailors

There wasn't enough business in villages so tailors, since at least the eleventh century, generally wielded their needles in towns. Essentially, a tailor made, altered and mended coats and jackets for men and women, and trousers and shirts for men.

Conditions did not change in the sixty years between Thomas Hood's *Song of the Shirt* and Charles Booth's extensive *Life and Labour of the People in London*, published in 1902–03, associating the trades of tailoring (and shoemaking) with poverty. Booth made a strong distinction between a journeyman working for a respectable West End London business and the 'wholesale contractor', the slopman, living and working with wife and children in one room with bad sanitation. Both tailors had undertaken an apprenticeship. According to Booth, a suit made by the respectable journeyman lasted forever whereas the other blew up 'like a balloon in the wind' and was unwearable within a few weeks. Booth did not take into account those unable to afford better-made clothing.

He included a table itemising rates and hours expected by various levels of tailors working from home. A routine working day was thirteen to fourteen hours, although some jobs were 'infinite'; the day ended when work was finished. A tailor-baster making three to four coats a day was the highest paid, receiving seven to nine shillings. The sewing machine, usually hired, was on the never-never. Payment, like rent, was collected weekly.

On the other hand, the West End journeyman piece-working in 1900 on the Society of Amalgamated Tailors' rates earned, depending on his skill, £2 10s a week in the high season, averaging £1–£2 a week over the year. London's season consisted of balls and social events and a new costume was made in a few days or overnight.

John Raymond, a witness at the murder trial of James Mullins and Walter Emm in 1860 describes himself thus: 'I am a tailor by business and reside at 12 Oxford Square (London)… a journeyman tailor, not a jobbing tailor – I am a coat maker – I work for Mr James Cook, of 63 Shoreditch…. I worked for Stevens and Clark – I have not been working for anybody since'. This detail for a journeyman is unusual and with this a family historian could investigate the employers; the more famous tailoring companies have more available information.

Using the free search of Merchant Taylors membership index 1530–1928 at **www.parishregister.com** and typing in John Raymond's name, there are two hits; John Raymond and John Rayment, but no date or further information. For £3.95, you might get the date of freedom by apprenticeship, patrimony or redemption; if apprenticeship, the name of his master; date of election to livery i.e. the Merchant Taylors' Company and any remarks. The Index of Freemen, compiled around 1930 and transcribed and published by Docklands Ancestors Ltd, contains 36,000 names and can be bought as a CD for £29.95. The results are either posted within twenty-one days or emailed. The Merchant Taylors' Company **www.merchant-taylors.co.uk** get a percentage of all purchases. The index can be viewed for free at Guildhall Library at MS 34037/1-4.

As always, go to your local record office first. The Shropshire Record Office has a register book for 1620–1771 (ref 6001/5837) for the Shrewsbury Company of Tailors and Skinners. Essex Records Office has records dating from 1572 including sessions rolls, writs, statute staple bonds and wills.

The V&A Museum has an extensive reading list of books and magazines on its website about the history of clothes and fashion from the sixteenth to twentieth centuries including pattern books. See **www.vam.ac.uk/content/articles/t/reading-list-tailoring**. Amazon has others.

The Working Class Movement Library in Salford **www.wcml.org.uk** has annual reports from the Amalgamated Society of Journeymen Tailors (later the Amalgamated Society of Tailors and Tailoresses) for 1870 to 1931, including obituaries for both members and wives, sick pay and benefits as well as roughly ten years of annual reports for the Amalgamated Society of Clothiers' Operatives dated 1894 to 1909.

Dressmakers and Seamstresses

Dressmaker is a common occupation for women in the census; not including ancillary occupations, 195,754 are listed for 1881 in England. They custom-made, repaired and altered dresses, blouses and evening gowns. A few are listed as 'dressmaker milliners' and were obviously responsible for the 'whole package'. The seamstress made, for instance, blouses. During the Edwardian penchant for tightly tucked and elaborate pleats selling for eighteen to twenty-five shillings each, she stitched up to a dozen blouses a week for ten shillings.

Dressmaking was more respectable than working in a factory but, because of cheap cloth manufactured in mills, women demanded correspondingly cheap garments, resulting in appallingly long hours for dressmakers and seamstresses. Twelve-year-old apprentices worked late into the night without pay. The official fifty-nine hour working week was overridden by women taking work home to finish.

Thomas Hood's 1843 poem *The Song of the Shirt*, which scandalised the middle and upper classes and depicted a respectable woman with failing eyesight freezing in a garret, was no exaggeration. For middle-class women who had fallen on hard times, dressmaking and seamstressing was the only suitable work offering independence. The alternative was being a governess or

Unknown lady wearing walking costume with silk jacket or paletot, c.1860s. Looking uncomfortable, has she borrowed the costume for the photograph or is it the first time she's worn it? Taken in a Newport Pagnell studio, this is from the family album. (Author's collection, ©Adèle Emm)

teaching (many women didn't have enough education for this), or becoming a servant or prostitute. For a woman who had employed servants of her own, working in service was untenable and a middle-class woman was unlikely to employ her anyway. The conjecture on various websites that 'dressmaker/seamstress' was a euphemism for prostitute is usually wrong. However destitute a woman might have been, in most cases a dressmaker was exactly that – a dressmaker.

Sewing machines were in general use from the middle of the 1850s in the UK (slightly earlier in the USA and Germany) with a patent 'sewing machine war' throughout the 1850s. Originally founded by William Jones and Thomas Chadwick in 1860, the Jones Sewing Machine Company had a huge factory in Guide Bridge near Manchester from 1869. The sewing machine revolutionised both shoemaking and dressmaking/tailoring industries, but not for the better, as wages decreased considerably. In the 1860s, 15,000 girls were employed by London dressmakers, working in appalling conditions for ten hours at a time and often eating and sleeping in the workrooms.

The Textiles Society **www.textilesociety.org.uk/textile-links/museums.php** has links to costume museums, organisations and online resources such as the London Sewing Machine Museum, the Embroiderer's Guild and the Crafts Study Centre.

Hat Making

My grandmother, like every woman of her generation, never went out without hat and gloves. Photos prior to the 1950s show everyone wearing a hat, be it cloth cap, Homburg, bowler, top hat or stylish millinery confection. In 1571, to promote the English wool trade, a law decreed that all non-noble Englishmen should wear wool caps, nicknamed 'statute caps', on Sundays and holidays. Lords and ladies were exempt. Hats were one of the few items during the Second World War which were not rationed.

Hats, like shoes, did not merely protect people against the elements, but were also safety wear (an equestrian sports a sunhat

Detail from postcard of Twin Wells, Lisdoonvarna, Co. Clare, Ireland, sent 1909. Everyone is wearing hats: straw, caps and more formal designs. (Author's collection ©Adèle Emm)

in the Elgin Marbles), a social or fashion statement or statement of power (crowns, flamboyant headdresses and so on). After the Second World War, the rise in popularity and convenience of the 'runabout', its decreasing cost (in 1929 a Crossley car cost, at £495, about the same as a suburban semi in Manchester) together with the introduction of radiators in the family car (during the 1960s) ensured the day of the hat was over.

The patron saint of felt makers and thereby hat makers is St Clement (died circa 100 AD). An unsubstantiated fanciful story is that he invented felt when, while a wandering monk, he placed some wool in his sandals to protect his sore feet. The rubbing and sweat turned the wool to felt.

Hatting required a supply of fur; beaver for the expensive hard-wearing hats, wool for cheaper ones. Hatting also required a supply of water for felt making and fuel for heating the water. In medieval times, London's Southwark was central to the industry, with access to both the moneyed classes and imported beaver. In Chester, a Guild of Feltmakers existed from 1550. Hatters were found in ports like Bristol, Exeter and Liverpool, with access to beaver, which was extinct in the UK by the sixteenth century. The *Book of Trades* of 1806

Hatter's bow at Stockport's Hat Works. (Courtesy of Stockport Metropolitan Museum, ©Adèle Emm)

recommended the craft 'as good a one that is practiced', adding that a journeyman could expect two guineas a week.

By the 1750s, beaver, by now virtually extinct worldwide, was extremely expensive so rabbit and wool was the norm. Luton (see straw hat making) and Warwickshire were significant hat centres, but the most important were Stockport and Denton near Manchester; Stockport County football club is still nicknamed the Hatters. Here, the hat making industry began in the sixteenth and seventeenth century when farmers supplemented their income making felt hats from wool or rabbit in a workshop attached to their farm. Initially these hats were sold locally and any surplus sent to London dealers.

In beaver hat making, the first procedure was for women to scrape away (developing lung congestion) the two types of beaver fur from the pelt, mixing them together whilst the dust and filth fell through slits in the table. In Stockport, rabbit fur was cleaned by using a hatter's bow, a contraption about seven feet long made from ash with a catgut string. Vibrations from the string separated hair from filth, which fell away simultaneously creating a film of evenly distributed fur several inches thick. This was pressed down to produce a large cone of floppy material – the hood – which was taken to a large basin with a wooden surround, the planking kettle, where hatters turned the hoods into felt by scrubbing them in a mixture of oatmeal, beer and nitric acid (including mercury) heated to about 60° Fahrenheit. Although hands were protected by leather guards, the constant soaking in acidic water resulted in skin erosion and soft, deformed hands.

An alternative method to the planking kettle was to soak the fur in the same noxious solution of nitric acid, beer and mercury, seal it in boxes and turn them every few hours. Whichever method, it was this use of mercury which resulted in poisoning, immortalised in the expression 'mad as a hatter' and *Alice in Wonderland*'s Mad Hatter. The symptoms were tremors, memory loss, paralysis, hallucinations, insanity and finally death. William Farr (1807–83), superintendent of the statistical department of the registrar-general, compiled

Planking kettle at Stockport's Hat Works. (Courtesy of Stockport Metropolitan Museum, ©Adèle Emm)

mortality rate statistics and claimed the average life expectancy of a Luton hatter was thirty-six and three quarter years.

The last surviving bow garret with two of its original windows is in Denton. Bow garrets operated from around 1790, before hat making became part of the factory system in the 1830s. Like all garrets it was isolated in a field until, over the years, housing was built around it. Unlike others, this was two storeys; the upper floor with better light housed the hatter's bow and the planking kettle was based on the ground floor.

Using wooden moulds called blocks, the hood was shrunk and

Reputedly the only surviving bow garret in the country, this listed building is in Denton near Stockport and still has its original windows. The upper floor housed the hatter's bow, while the planking kettle was on the ground floor. (©Adèle Emm)

thickened in the planking kettle, then shaped and bullied into a hat. Different sized blocks were required for different head sizes, with a different block for each hat style. Tied to its block, several hats were dyed together. The recipe given in the *Book of Trades* describes the lethal combination of gum, verdigris and vitriol. After an hour or more, they were taken out and dried and more hats dyed. Once dry, hats were stiffened with gum, hand steamed and brushed until glossy. Finally, they were ironed and trimmed. In the factory system, finishing was a woman's job where, using sewing machines, trimmings, decoration and manufacturers' labels were added.

The first Christys' hat making factory was in Bermondsey, London, but in 1824 they set up a factory in Stockport. Other companies followed. Wages were considerably lower here; strict regulations concerning apprenticeships did not generally apply in the provinces and Stockport already had a reputation for hatters working their own 'hat shops'. Stockport hats were sold around the world.

The 1840s saw a crisis in the hatting industry. The fashion for top hats made not of felt but silk, meant hundreds of hatters were unemployed. Much cheaper to make and buy, top hats were accessible to everyone down to the poor man in the street, including the Artful Dodger in *Oliver Twist*. Reputedly brought to England from France in 1797 by London haberdasher John Hetherington, who caused a disturbance of the peace by wearing it, Christys' made them in Stockport from 1849. To challenge its supremacy, the wideawake hat (circa 1840), a soft floppy hat as unlike the stiff top hat as possible, was introduced. It earned its soubriquet because it had no nap (material's fuzzy surface), a pun on not sleeping, hence wide awake. With a wide brim and soft crown it was also known as a 'billycock' and was popular with the middle and working classes. A machine, invented by William Barber to shape the soft fur billycock hats, was used in Christys' from the 1850s. The wideawake was still sported by Boy Scouts in 1903.

It was a wideawake or billycock that was partly responsible for convicting plasterer James Mullins of murder in 1860 (see Chapter

150

8). Mullins wore his wideawake as a symbol of his occupation. A witness at the trial, seaman John Mitchell, said, 'you would have been alarmed if you had been here – he had on corduroy trousers, a brown wide-awake, and a kind of a drab tweed coat, with shooting pockets.' Mullins' hat was probably made in Stockport.

The bowler hat (often erroneously called a billycock) was devised by James Lock in 1849 (see Chapter 5) for William Coke, the Earl of Leicester, who wanted an indestructible hat which could withstand knocks by trees and protect his gamekeepers. The story goes that William Coke jumped on the shellac domed hat and, as it wasn't crushed, bought it. When it went into production, 60,000 'Bowlers' or 'Cokes' as they are also known, were made each year. Lock's records are held at the LMA.

In 1860, 700 hatters lived in Stockport and there were fifty-three hatting firms. By 1885, this had increased to more than 8,000 hatters living and working either in factories or their own hat shop (workshop). By 1892, there were thirty hat factories in the area including Battersby's, Carringtons, Christys', T.W. Lees and Moores, supplying hats all around the world. After the First World War, in January 1919, there was a shortage of labour and the hatting industry was unable to meet demand. By the end of the year there was a glut of labour. Sadly, in 1997, the last hatting company, Christys', moved out of Stockport, although the company still makes top hats and bowlers in Britain.

Alongside all prominent industries are ancillary trades. In the hat industry, this included, among other things, block making (the factory system used hundreds of different ones), hat-box production, trimming materials such as bows and lace, hat pin makers and engineering companies building machinery for hat factories together with tanners, curriers, felt makers and the fur and wool trade.

Hatting unions were strong during the 1880s and 1890s and there were many different ones e.g. the Society of Journeyman Hatters in Denton (1872) and the Amalgamated Felt Hat Trimmers' Wool Formers' and Allied Workers Union still in existence in the 1940s. Christys' in Stockport refused to admit unions until the First World

Assorted hat blocks at Stockport's Hat Works. (Courtesy of Stockport Metropolitan Museum, ©Adèle Emm)

War. For finding trade union members see Mark Crail's excellent *Tracing your Labour Movement Ancestors*. Guildhall Library is useful for London hatters. If your ancestors were involved in strikes such as Denton in 1841 and the early nineteenth century, you may find references to them in local newspapers.

The Worshipful Company of Feltmakers, founded 1604 (preceded by the Company of Cappers 1269 and later incorporated with the Haberdashers), still annually presents the incoming Lord Mayor of London with a tricorne hat. Their records are at Guildhall. A hatter's apprenticeship lasted seven years and, according to the 1667 regulations of the Feltmakers' Company in London, a hatter could only employ two apprentices per master. For a journeyman hatter to become a full hatter, they made a masterpiece hat one-sixth the size of a normal one; similar miniature hats were touted around by travelling salesmen as demonstration hats.

A volunteer feltmaking list has related sites (many abroad), including how to make felt and felt goods on **http://members. peak.org/~spark/feltlistFAQ.html**. The following mailing list has a link to British hatters, among others: **www.rootsweb.ancestry. com/~jfuller/gen_mail_occ.html**.

The procedure for making hats in both an individual hat maker's shop, the factory system and by machinery is explained and demonstrated at the excellent Stockport Hatting Museum **www.stockport.gov.uk/hatworks**, the only museum in the country solely dedicated to hats and hatting. Although some indentures for the Stockport area are held at the Museum, they contain little of biographical interest. The Museum holds a small collection of relevant hat making books and *Hatters' Gazette*, wonderful for general hatting background but with little biographical information. You must make an appointment. Stockport Local Heritage Library **www.stockport.gov.uk** holds Christys', Battersby, Sutton and Torkington archives as well as Ordnance Surveys from 1849 onwards and a photographic library. Luton's Wardown Park Museum, closed for refurbishment until at least 2016, has some hat galleries. Like Stockport's Hat Museum, they have copies of *Hatters' Gazette* and

The Luton News but little biographical information. Luton Central Library may also have background information.

Straw Hat Making

Iris in Act IV of Shakespeare's *The Tempest* says, 'Make holiday, your rye-straw hats put on.' Summer hats were cool, light and often of straw.

According to Harry Inwards' *Straw Hats, their History and Manufacture*, published 1922, the straw hat industry dates from roughly the reign of James I (1603–25) and is largely centred around Bedfordshire, Hertfordshire and East Buckinghamshire. In around 1689, Luton, objecting to foreign imports of straw and straw hats from Italy, petitioned the government, claiming 14,000 people earned a living making straw hats. The importance of Luton's straw industry is evidenced by Plait Halls, now demolished, being their first covered market hall. Luton's House of Maintenance, a euphemistic term for the workhouse, taught straw plaiting and hat-making to its inmates and, after the First World War, Luton had virtually overtaken Stockport for cheap woollen felt hats using improved machines. The decline of the straw hat industry was partly due to changes in fashion and the war between Japan and China, which made it difficult to import raw materials.

According to *The Book of Trades* 1806, straw hat making required little monetary capital, with one guinea enough to purchase enough straw and machinery for several months for a workforce of a hundred. This trade is the first in the book depicting women as the workforce.

The straw, preferably rye or wheat, is plaited before being made up into a hat. Bundles of straw were cut into lengths of eight to ten inches and about ten inches in circumference. They were dipped in water before being placed in boxes containing brimstone, a caustic type of sulphur, which was set on fire to smoke the straw. One person selected straws for up to fifty bonnet makers who plaited them using thumb and second finger. It was fiddly work and the straw had to be constantly moistened, usually with saliva, so girls had chapped lips, sore fingers and medical problems from imbibing sulphur. Once the plait was five yards long (just over four and a half meters), it was wound around a wooden template and left there for several days. A good plaiter made sixty a week. Once plaited, they were sewn into bonnets or hats, usually by women working from home; the style depended on contemporary fashion. To finish, the hat or bonnet was put on a block similar to those in felt hat making and pressed. Sulphur was used to make hats whiter in colour. Women in 1806 earned about half a guinea a week, with plaiters earning more. It was not a lot, but this doubled a family income when an agricultural labourer earned less at eight to ten shillings a week.

The 1851 census for Newport Pagnell highlights different occupations in the straw hat industry: ten people were involved in straw and straw bonnet manufacturing (mainly but not exclusively men); but there were nine bonnet and hat sewers and eight straw bonnet makers, all women – not including those in the workhouse. Most women working as straw bonnet workers had husbands or fathers in trade; cooper, butcher, journeyman carpenter. One family was headed by a spinster with this as their main income. Any basket makers recorded, who presumably used the same source of straw and reed, were men.

Wing, Buckinghamshire, had a vibrant straw plaiting industry. Records for the same 1851 census show nineteen per cent of children under ten were straw plaiters and thirty-six per cent of adult women were involved in the same industry. More information can be found at **www.wing-ops.org.uk/straw.html**.

By the late 1800s, cheap imports from the Far East resulted in a serious decline in the straw plaiting industry. In 1903, straw plaits were sold at a penny and three farthings to six pence a yard depending on quality. Most came from abroad and women diversified to include millinery in their repertoire, as evidenced by the census records.

Because there was no organisation or livery company attached to this industry, there are no apprentice records. Any available records are in local record offices.

Milliners

Milliners made ladies' hats, but many provided a full service including dress making and muffs. They were plentiful in towns and cities; Kelly's 1928 *Directory* lists forty-seven in Buckinghamshire; two in Newport Pagnell and four in Wolverton. Local newspapers and directories plus record offices might reveal more about your ancestor.

In 1908, Amy Reeve published *Practical Home Millinery*, explaining the methods of hat production from cutting the pattern from paper to fit the individual customer, to making wire frames and trimmings such as bows, rosettes and feathers. Like a recipe book, it listed 'ingredients' as well as method.

Button Makers

Button making was originally a cottage industry similar to lace making and, to a certain extent, straw plaiting. Although found virtually everywhere, some areas were more important than others. Macclesfield, a silk weaving centre, produced silk buttons from at least the sixteenth century with poor children taught the craft from 1698. Merchants bought materials wholesale and distributed it to families to make buttons at home. Wooden bases were covered with material and, using a needle, silk and mohair were woven and threaded on to them. A 'diligent woman' could earn four shillings a week. In 1693, during the reign of William and Mary, it was illegal to import buttons made with hair and, six years later, a further Act protected the thousands of mainly women and children English button makers.

Fashions change. By the reign of George III, coats and jackets were festooned with gilt and metal buttons and the constant wars ensured demand. About this time, Birmingham became a significant

Son of a prosperous Newport Pagnell baker, c.1906. This boy wears a lace collar, military-style metal buttons and well-made shoes. (Author's collection, ©Adèle Emm)

centre for button making (also buckles and toys) with several button manufacturers specialising in metal buttons for military uniforms. By 1759, it was estimated that around 20,000 people worked in the industry. If your ancestor claimed button maker as their occupation they may have worked in a factory, perhaps for John Taylor (died 1775) who gilded buttons, John Lee, Samuel Hammond (died 1825) or Matthew Boulton (died 1809). Georgian fashionistas wanted metal button bases covered with gold leaf or plated with silver. By the end of the eighteenth century a cheaper method was invented whereby buttons were dipped, producing a thinner and cheaper layer of precious metal.

It was not difficult work as the process was like a production line; each button travelled many hands before completion. In the 1800s, a twelve-year-old girl's job was to 'put in shanks' with working hours of 8am to 7.45pm. Boys aged nine to twelve cracked corozo nuts in an outhouse and children could earn ten pence to eight shillings a week. Corozo palm tree nuts were similar in texture to ivory.

Factory work was unpleasant and dangerous; health and safety was minimal. Machines were powered by steam and the *Birmingham Gazette* reported several unpleasant accidents at Hammond Turner & Sons, which employed over 200 workers in the Snow Hill area. A nineteen-year-old youth died after his arm was mangled by a circular saw; another boy's clothes were caught in a flywheel.

Birmingham also specialised in mother-of-pearl buttons, a cottage industry operating outside the factory system. At the end of the eighteenth century, the government banned the import of pearl buttons to protect the home industry. Because of the fragile nature of nacre, the shell from which mother-of-pearl buttons were made, the technique was less mechanised than for other buttons. The only equipment required was a foot lathe.

The shells were imported from the East Indies and the Pacific Ocean, often by large manufacturers who distributed them to outworkers to make the buttons. The shells were sorted, cut into buttons, holes drilled for the thread and finally polished. These men were highly skilled and could earn £2 to £4 a week; a fortune compared to women in the factories earning seven to nine shillings a week. It was often a family-run operation in squalid conditions, with members taking on different roles. Once completed, the buttons were sewn on to cards to sell at the haberdasher. A factory girl could sew 3,600 buttons on a card a day!

The Dorset shirt button industry was established near Shaftesbury and Blandford, although stitched buttons had been produced in Dorset since the sixteenth century. In 1622 Abraham Case organised home workers in the area. In 1731, Robert Fisher opened a button depot in Blandford Forum where outworkers brought their work for him to sell. Originally, the button base was made of Dorset sheep horn covered in cloth and overworked with thread. Later, metal rings from Birmingham were used. By 1793, nearly 4,000 women and children as young as six were employed around Dorset. The children 'cast' the buttons by covering the base with wire, at which point the more experienced adult 'filled' the button by winding thread around it into different styles and patterns. A skilled woman produced twelve dozen a day, although the average was seven dozen, and in 1812 she could earn between six shillings and twelve shillings a week. A woman working in the fields earned no more than nine pence a day – about four shillings and six pence a week. Making buttons, she was earning more and indoors where conditions were better.

Again, fashions change and by mid-Victorian England button makers' income was reduced to under three shillings a week. When a button-making machine was exhibited at the Great Exhibition in Crystal Palace in 1851, the effect was immediate. By 1860, the button industry had collapsed, leaving many destitute.

Records for homeworking button makers, like lacemakers, are sparse and difficult to locate simply because records weren't kept. First stop is the local record office such as Dorset **www.dorsetforyou.com/dorsethistorycentre**, which has relevant books and some archives. For additional information on button making in this area see **www.thedorsetpage.com/history/Button_Making/**

button_making.htm. Some towns and villages have websites outlining local occupations, occasionally including information on families and names of people involved. A Google search should reveal them. The British Button Society for collectors has a website **www.chezfred.org.uk/bbs**, which may be of general interest and links to an eclectic mix of buttonalia sites.

Glovers

In medieval times, gloves, a significant symbol of social class, were given as a present, especially to a lover. A few years later and we meet perhaps the most famous glover and whittawer (leather worker) in history, John Shakespeare (1531–1601) and, by association, his son William. Because they were essentially leather workers, cordwainers also made gloves (see Chapter 8).

The industry was concentrated where there was a plentiful supply of cattle and sheep, with most gloves made from calf or sheepskin. Deer was occasionally used and kid gloves, highly prized and expensive, came from goat. The leather grain was inside and fur lining added for warmth; the outside was stained. Depending on fashion, gloves could be made from satin, silk and velvet and were often extremely elaborate with lace, beads and fringing.

During medieval manufacture, leather was treated with alum, making it pale but not particularly supple; the skill was to make gloves fit the hands but supple enough to provide movement. Several processes were involved, from preparing skins to staining and cutting. By 1862, it was somewhat of a production line with both men and women working at different stages; an explanation of the processes in glove making is in the chapter 'Mr Ashley's Manufactory' in *Mrs Halliburton's Troubles* by Mrs Henry Wood, 1862, found free online.

In order to preserve employment, imported gloves were prohibited during the reigns of Richard I, Edward IV and Elizabeth I. The penalty for importing, selling or owning imported gloves during the reign of George III was the enormous sum of £200, with the contraband sold by auction under the peculiar terms of 'the candle' – the sale lasted as long as it took for an inch-long candle to burn. Whoever was bidding when the light went out got the goods! Predictably, gloves were smuggled alongside brandy, lace and tea. In 1766, anyone owning imported goods could be fined £20 plus three times the value of the gloves. In 1785, gloves were taxed on a sliding scale starting at one penny per pair of gloves selling at between four and ten pence a pair, with revenue collected at the point of sale. Nine years later, the tax was repealed for bringing in too little revenue.

All trade restrictions for the import of leather and material were removed in 1826 resulting in catastrophe for English glove makers. At first, everyone flocked to glove making centres and for a while a lot of money was made – £1 to £1 ten shillings a week was common – until it was realised more gloves were made than sold. Working hours were slashed alongside wages; women earned four pence a day and men eight pence a day. Unemployed glovers packed the workhouses and by 1831 there were only 1,615 male glovers over the age of twenty working in the UK **www.histpop.org**. The situation improved slightly by 1841 with 9,000 (including silk glove makers), virtually half of them – 4,295 – were women. Ten years later, this had increased to 29,882 but fell each decade to 16,811 by 1871. The rot was irreversible. Machines were cutting and sewing gloves from the mid-nineteenth century and in the 1880s could perform most processes apart from hemming the welt on the opening of the gloves. In the 1881 census for England, Wales and Scotland (FindMyPast) there were a mere 5,661 glovers.

Worcester and its surrounding villages formed a major glove making centre from at least 1571. Between 1790 and 1820, half the glovers in Britain were based around Worcester with 30,000 people working for 150 manufacturers. Perhaps the most famous glove company was Dent, Allcroft and Co., which employed thousands of glove sewers, sending transport fifty miles around to collect finished articles from workers in their own homes. Their records for 1781–1853 are held privately at Gloucester Archives; contact them for access. Founded in London in 1877, the Fownes Glove Company relocated to Worcester in 1887, employing more than 1,000 people.

The Worshipful Company of Glovers **www.theglovers company.org**, founded in London in 1349, is sixty-second in the order of preference. To ensure their customers weren't swindled, a glove seller had to sell their wares by daylight, not candlelight, so the quality could be more easily inspected. Reflecting their plight, there were 120 in the Company in the first half of the eighteenth century, but only fourteen by the end. Their archives are at Guildhall Library. Their historic glove collection is on permanent loan to Bath Fashion Museum and viewable online at **www.glovecollection catalogue.org**.

Another guild involved in the glove trade was the Company of Fellmongers, originally the Glovers and Skinners Companies. A fell was the sheep's pelt and the fellmonger separated the wool from the hide, selling it to the glove-making trade. The website of the Fellmongers Company, Richmond, Yorkshire **www.fellmongers. org.uk** has relevant photographs for their trade. Their minute books have been rediscovered; one in a university in New York and the other at a Sotheby's auction in 1980, and the archives can be visited at York.

For glovers outside London, try the local records centre; for instance the Shropshire Record Office has a register book of the Glovers' Company with records for 1638–1817. The Northampton Shoe and Boot Museum has leather craft information, although generally not genealogical. Be prepared for disappointment.

Lacemaking

According to legend, lace was brought to England by Henry VIII's first wife Catherine of Aragon (1485–1536), although few believe this to be true. Lace was popular from the late Tudor period (one of Queen Elizabeth I's ruffs reputedly cost £3,000), but its favour depended on fashion. Queen Victoria's wedding dress and her son's

Variety Hall favourite Marie Studholme, wearing elaborate lace cap and blouse. Postcard dated 1906. (Author's collection, ©Adèle Emm)

christening gown, later worn by princes William and Harry, was made of Honiton lace, making it chic in the mid-1800s.

Hand-made lace making was important in Nottingham, Bedfordshire, Buckinghamshire and Devon, especially around

Honiton. Newport Pagnell's wealth and fine Georgian houses in the High Street are attributable to its lacemaking industry from the seventeenth to nineteenth centuries.

There are two techniques for hand-made lace; bobbin lace and needlepoint. Bobbin lace uses cards on which the pattern is pricked out and a bewildering number of bobbins are moved to create the design. The needles for the pattern were stuck into a 'pillow,' a large cushion stuffed with horsehair or straw until it was packed tight, and the bobbins wound around them whilst the pillow rested on a three-legged stool called a horse. Bobbin lace made in Newport Pagnell was Bucks Point, named after the county but not exclusive to it.

Needlepoint uses a needle and one thread, a bit like crochet, and is regarded as a quicker form of lace making.

In the 1851 census, there were over 250 lacemakers, all women, listed as working in Newport Pagnell, not including those in the workhouse. With over 3,600 people, this equates to nearly seven per cent of the population. In addition, there was a lace dealer and grocer (male) who presumably pursued both occupations to make a living.

According to a letter from local poet William Cowper in July 1790, the nearby 'beggarly' town of Olney had 1,200 lacemakers out of a population of 2,000; sixty per cent of the town eked a living from lace and, according to Cowper, they were distressingly poor. Queen Victoria had yet to make lace fashionable again. Links to the Buckinghamshire lace industry can be found on **www.mkheritage. co.uk**.

In neighbouring Bedfordshire, lacemaker burials from parish registers 1717–1809 for Turvey are listed online at **www. turveybeds.com/lacemaking.html**. Young children were taught to make lace, but not necessarily literacy, at the school in Newton Lane and such schools were common in the eighteenth and early nineteenth centuries.

Like their counterparts in Buckinghamshire and Bedfordshire, Devon lacemakers, wives of labourers and fishermen, supplemented the family income by making lace at home and selling it to agents and shop owners.

Nottingham's lace trade was centred on the Lace Market, with salerooms and warehouses housing lace made in local factories or brought in from outworkers. From as early as 1800, this trade was warehouse and factory based, with twelve-hour working days six days a week, extended to Sundays during busy periods. Apart from 'finishing' work, most employees were men and the machine work was regarded as so physically demanding that boys under fourteen were generally not employed from 1833. Their apprenticeship usually lasted seven years and, in the early 1900s, boys could earn thirty-three shillings a week, whereas a bank trainee might only receive ten shillings. The outworkers, mainly women, worked under appalling conditions at home finishing the lace. An outworker mistress collected work from the warehouse, for which she was given a fixed price. She then distributed the work amongst other women, who often engaged their families and children as young as eight (younger before the 1860s) to mend, separate nets and cut off loose threads before returning the work to the mistress to collect the pay. Although the work was undertaken in miserable conditions, it was regarded as better than working in a factory. In 1873, a fifty-two hour working week was considered short.

Because of the hours spent inside (country homeworkers sat outside on summer days), lacemakers were pale and unhealthy with poor eyesight, stooped from working over lace from so young for so many hours. Tuberculosis was common.

The Industrial Revolution introduced machine-made lace and by 1900 most hand-made lace had disappeared.

Finding specific information about a lacemaker ancestor is difficult. Although lacemaking in its heyday paid more than an agricultural labourer earning eleven shillings a week in the 1850s down to seven in the 1870s recession, it was a cottage industry without formal apprenticeships and no written records, carried out largely by women (Newport Pagnell parish registers list a few male lacemakers) who, because of their lowly status and the poor recognition of lacemaking, are often unrecorded.

If you have ancestors who were lacemakers, try searching the name of their village to find a dedicated website where you might find helpful information about your family. If your lacemaking ancestors hail from Devon, Kirsty Gray's *Tracing your West Country Ancestors* (Pen and Sword, 2013) has an excellent bibliography and suggestions of relevant West Country websites.

Notwithstanding the time required to fashion it and therefore its prohibitive cost, modern hand-made lace is still made by devotees in Olney, Buckinghamshire **www.olneylacecircle.co.uk** and by the Lace Guild **www.laceguild.org** based in Stourbridge. They have a collection of over 15,000 objects relating to lace making including bobbins, netting needles and lace samples. Their website has videos on how lace is made and explains its history.

Places to Visit

• Many museums have displays of clothing and accessories. These are a selection; you may need an appointment to visit some specialist collections.
• The Bowes Museum Fashion and Textile Gallery, Barnard Castle, County Durham **www.thebowesmuseum.org.uk**; wide collection of costumes and textiles and the Blackborne lace collection.
• Costume and Textile Association, Norwich, **www.ctacostume. org.uk**; collection of shawls representing the textile trade in Norwich.
• Cowper and Newton Museum, Olney, Bucks **www.cowper andnewtonmuseum.org.uk**; explanation of lace making and local examples.
• Fashion Museum, Bath, **http://www.museumofcostume.co.uk** plus collection of gloves **www.glovecollectioncatalogue.org**
• Hope House Costume Museum and Restoration, Hope House, Alstonefield, Derbyshire **www.hopehousemuseum.co.uk**; appointment only.
• The Lace Guild, Stourbridge, **www.laceguild.org**; visits by prior arrangement.
• Museum of London **www.museumoflondon.org.uk**; varied

collection of clothing and accessories; 2,500 buttons collected over thirty years from the River Thames by mudlark Tony Pilson, in storage but viewable online **http://collections.museumoflondon. org.uk/online/searchresults.aspx?description=2009.33&newAdv Search=true**.

• Platt Hall Gallery of Costume, Manchester, **www.manchester galleries.org/our-other-venues/platt-hall-gallery-of-costume**; clothing and accessories from around 1600; Alan and Gillian Meredith's button collection of over 100,000 buttons dating from circa 1500. The collection is online.

• Stockport Hat Works **www.stockport.gov.uk/hatworks**.

• Waddesdon Manor, Aylesbury, Buckinghamshire, **www. waddesdon.org.uk**; costume and accessories, lace (not English) and 600 buttons.

• York Castle Museum; fans, shawls, underwear and clothing from ordinary people; **www.yorkcastlemuseum.org.uk/Page/View Collection.aspx?CollectionId=8**

• V&A Museum **www.vam.ac.uk**.

Chapter 10
OTHER TRADES

We cannot all be masters.
Iago, *Othello*, Shakespeare

Coopers

The highly skilled wet cooper (Latin, *cuparius/cupa–* cask) made barrels, casks, kegs and tuns for liquids, especially beer. A white cooper produced churns, tubs and pails for daily use and a dry cooper made barrels for flour, herring and gunpowder – think Gunpowder Plot, 1605. Casks are made in different sizes, each with a specific name and capacity; a barrel contains thirty-four gallons (1688), a firkin nine gallons (1803), a kilderkin eighteen gallons (1803) and so on. The advantage of a barrel over other containers is that it withstands harsh treatment, holds liquids without leaking, is easily stacked and can be transported by rolling. The craft is an ancient skill: barrels are depicted in Egyptian tomb paintings circa 2,960 BCE and were used in England from at least the Iron Age. The Romans transported wine in barrels.

Travelling coopers in 1806, paid piecework, cried for work in London and journeyed through the countryside carrying different sized hoops, iron rivets, wooden pegs and tools to make repairs. For an extra penny or two, they took on the work of a village carpenter; it was, after all, another form of wood working. A journeyman cooper could receive three to five shillings a day. King's coopers were employed at custom houses to maintain the alcohol barrels.

Bristol apprentice indentures 1554–1646 itemise a cooper's kit to include: addes (adze), howel, barge axe, hatchet, creves or croze which cut the groove (the eponymous *croze*) on the inside of a barrel,

Cheeky Edwardian postcard of a drunk enjoying the fruits of a barrel. (Author's collection, ©Adèle Emm)

compass, wimble (brace), saw, jointer and lave (lathe). Many tools were similar to those used by carpenters, but others were specific to coopering e.g. a spokeshave and a knocker up, a bent iron bar poked through the bung hole to ram the top cask head into place. The only time a cooper used a measuring tool was to make the heads (the lids); all other measurements were by eye.

In *The Book of Trades* 1806, the preferred wood was American oak seasoned (dried) for up to two years, cut into thin strips called staves and either kept straight or bent depending on its later purpose. For buckets, where the circumference of the bottom is smaller than the top, staves are wider at the top. The hoops, hence the surname Hooper, held the staves together around the outside circumference and were made of hazel and ash harvested from coppices or metal depending on the subsequent use of the barrel. A strip of reed (flag) placed between each stave swelled when wet to produce a watertight barrel. The Guinness website at **www.guinness-storehouse.com/en/docs/Coopering_Process.pdf** has an excellent description of coopering including photographs.

By the beginning of the twentieth century, most coopering was for the beer and whisky industries. Once metal casks were introduced by Guinness in 1946, the cooper's trade virtually ceased although, according to Speyside Cooperage, a handful of specialists working today using traditional tools still repair 150,000 casks a year. Coopering demonstrations are occasionally held at craft fairs.

The Worshipful Company of Coopers **www.coopers-hall.co.uk** is thirty-sixth in the order of preference and is first mentioned in the Mayor's Court records in 1298 where three coopers are named and shamed for misdemeanours. The Company's collection of tools and artefacts is held at Coopers' Hall, open only to members, and includes correspondence, casks and memorabilia of the trade. It can be viewed online at **www.coopers-hall.co.uk/museum-gallery**. Although the medieval hall didn't escape the Great Fire of London, the records and plate had been removed to safety the previous day. The 1868 hall was destroyed in 1940 in the Blitz but the records, stored in a basement safe, survived and are now deposited in

Guildhall Library. A list of archives for 1440–1978, including financial accounts, lists of freemen, registers of apprentice bindings and records relating to charities are on the AIM25 website **www. aim25.ac.uk/cgi-bin/vcdf/detail?coll_id=14131&inst_ id=118**. For coopers apprenticed and working outside London your best bet is the local records office, but information is scattered and variable.

Printers, Bookbinders and Stationers

The earliest books were meticulously written manuscripts, illustrated, copied and bound by monks. So expensive and valued were they that they were chained up, as in Hereford Cathedral and Chetham's Library, Manchester. Made of vellum, they were bound to keep pages together in the correct order and, to keep pages flat, encompassed between boards – hard covers. When William Caxton (1422–91) set up his printing press in Westminster in 1476, binding and printing became two different occupations; printers printed, while binders bound books.

Considering the symbiotic relationship between books and monks, it isn't surprising to find fifteenth-century printers and booksellers based around London's St Paul's Cathedral and Paternoster Row. They constituted either small print shops in front of their houses or stalls open to the elements (healthy for books!) and, according to Thomas Symonds in 1514, were open for business from seven in the morning. It's a logical progression that, a mere stroll away, Fleet Street became the epicentre of the newspaper industry.

By the mid-1840s, booksellers and bookbinders had moved behind the Strand, as explained by George Reynolds in his *Mysteries of London 1844–46*.

> Holywell Street was once noted only as a mart for second-hand clothing, and booksellers' shops dealing in indecent prints and volumes. The reputation it thus acquired was not a very creditable one…

171

Several highly respectable booksellers and publishers have [now] located themselves in the place that once deserved no better denomination than Rag Fair. The reputation of Holywell Street has now ceased to be a by-word: it is respectable; and, as a mart for the sale of literary wares, threatens to rival Paternoster Row.

A law preventing sedition and blasphemy was passed in 1549, ensuring all books were examined before sale. Throughout history, printing has been deemed dangerous to the contemporary government (as today) and during periods of insurrection renegade printers were persecuted at pain of death. At such times, some presses were 'secret', although they made a veritable racket when in operation. Those printing political tracts were likely to be Nonconformists and it is worth checking Nonconformist sources to reveal more information.

To ensure compliance, printers were licenced, for example under the Unlawful Societies Act 1799, and an ancestor's licence may be in the public record office together with their registered press number. No licence, no work. No work, starvation.

Maximising opportunity during the Thames frost fairs of 1814, printers took their presses onto the ice, cranking out souvenirs. A journeyman printer, compositor or pressman in 1818 could earn, according to the *Book of Trades*, thirty shillings to two guineas a week.

The earliest paper, cloth parchment, was made in the thirteenth century from linen rags mixed with wood and straw, beaten to a pulp using copious amounts of water, pressed, dried and hardened. England's first rag paper mill was set up in 1588 by Queen Elizabeth I's jeweller, Sir John Spilman (?–1626) in Dartford, Kent, using the plentiful supply of water from the River Darent. Spilman/Spielman was a German employing German immigrants in his mill until English workers developed the skills and expertise. It produced good-quality white paper rather than the ubiquitous brown which was, apart from parchment and vellum, the only alternative. By the following year he had a monopoly on the production of white paper.

There *were* other mills; thirty-seven existed in England between 1588 and 1650, but all producing the inferior brown paper.

An impression of Spilman's mill is given in Thomas Churchyard's sycophantic 1588 poem:

> The Hammers thump and make so loud a noise
> As fuller doth that beats his woollen cloth
> In open show, then Sundry secret toyes
> Make rotten rags to yield a thickened froth
> There it is stamped and washed as white as snow
> Then flung on frame and hanged to dry, I trow
> Thus paper straight it is to write upon
> As it were rubbed and smoothed with slicking stone.

Hand-made paper was produced by dipping a metal fine-wire frame into the pulp, taken out and dried. Because of the wires, the paper contained lines, much like brown wrapping paper today. Over the years, the wires were spaced at different widths, which is how experts date old paper. Paper was subject to excise duty and tax from 1696 until 1861. In 1712, each paper mill was given an Excise number which, should the mill become redundant, was used again on another mill.

A machine invented in 1844 made paper from wood pulp, not rags, contributing to the nineteenth century's voracious appetite for newspapers and books. The Education Acts worked wonders on literacy levels, shown indirectly by census records; in 1851, there were 26,024 printers and by 1871 nearly twice as many at 44,814.

Newport Pagnell's William Cowley parchment works has been in existence since 1870 and is the only company in the UK still making commercial sheepskin parchment. Their website at **www.william cowley.co.uk** explains the processes employed in this industry. Parchment and vellum are made from skins and hides and, like paper making, need a constant supply of water for cleaning hides, which is why the industry was based near rivers. In the past, this industry, like other leather/hide based industries such as tanning, which used animal excrement to prepare the leather, was accompanied by a nauseating stench. Wealthier citizens lived upwind.

Bookbinders were generally located near the printer and proliferated in the late seventeenth century and early eighteenth century. The studio or workshop where book binding took place was the bindery, usually a workshop in the binder's house. It needed sewing frames and needles for stitching pages together, guillotines or sharp knives, stamps for engraving and indentations and a press to hold the book still whilst working on it, together with leather or cloth for covers, gold leaf and twine. Itinerant bookbinders travelled the country carrying their tools in packs.

In 1868, a bookbinding sewing machine was invented by David McConnell Smyth, followed by gluing, trimming and case-making (hard cover) machines. According to Walter Newbury, who set up his bookbinding company in 1895 in Plashett Grove, East Ham, 'the machine is but the servant of a good workman'. A perfectly bound book encompassed the essentials of solidity (so they didn't fall apart), elasticity (easily opened) and elegance as emphasised in Newbury's motto, 'thoroughness'.

Like many crafts, bookbinding suffered badly over the years although the trade was boosted by the highly elaborate and influential designs of William Morris (1834–1896). Their bread and butter now consists of restoration work and binding university theses.

As a commercial trade, printing, bookbinding and the stationery business was limited by literacy levels and, until the majority of people could read, the stationer traded to a highly sophisticated and prosperous customer in affluent areas such as a city or large town.

It was common in smaller towns to find booksellers and stationers incorporated within another trade. Anne Chapman, running a pharmacy and perfumery in Newport Pagnell in 1795, had a side-line in books, although there was a full-time bookseller in town.

As well as pen and ink, notepaper, envelopes, wrapping paper, sealing wax and string, stationers sold books intended to be written in: diaries, notebooks, account books and ledgers. These shops were a repository of scholarship and pensiveness, often doubling as private libraries where, for a subscription, books were borrowed with a fine for those returned late, lost or damaged. Books were relatively expensive so it was a cheap way to access a wider selection of books. After the rise of the public library from the early twentieth century and free book borrowing, private libraries fell out of favour, but there is always a silver lining for someone. Here it was the bookbinder whose trade was boosted by rebinding books in plain covers for the libraries.

British History Online has a fascinating explanation of the industry and mentions some London practitioners. It explains that these are the minority, as few bookbinders are known by name. If you have a bookbinder working in London, they may be mentioned in **www.british-history.ac.uk/report.aspx?compid=22177**. If your ancestors were papermakers in Exeter, Devon, try **http://book history.blogspot.co.uk**.

The British Library is attempting to compile a database of bookbinders **www.bl.uk/catalogues/bookbindings**. There is a small picture gallery of bindings throughout the ages and a search box where a name brings up any books in their library for which they have bookbinder information. 'Smith' brought up eighty-nine results including W. Smith of Iron Bridge (circa 1817), bound in brown calf and blind tooled. C. Smith worked in Bath around 1800 and one of his books is bound in black goatskin, tooled in gold. The advanced search lists all the bookbinders in their database. Results include a thumbnail of the book cover. Some books have considerable detail but, as this project is a work in progress, some records are incomplete.

A fraternity of stationers was in existence in 1404 and the Royal Charter for the Stationers' Company's was bestowed in 1557 when few could read. Not all early booksellers and printers belonged to this Company; some were members of the Grocers' and Drapers' Companies, so check there too. Gordon Duff's *A Century of the*

English Book Trade, 1905, **https://archive.org/details/centuryof english00duffuoft** names names and explains the English book trade in the fifteenth and sixteen centuries.

The British Book Trade Index at the University of Birmingham is a useful and easily negotiated resource at **www.bbti.bham.ac.uk**. As explained on the website, the information is compiled from various primary sources such as directories, poll books, census records and British Record Society indexes, and includes variations of names and occasional duplicate information. The index catalogues anyone working in the book trade, including Stationers' Company masters and apprentices, auctioneers, book sellers, binders, stationers, papermakers, publishers, printers, rag-makers and the like from the fifteenth century (there are not many of these). Some trades appear to have little relevance to the book trade itself, so check similar trades in your family; fellmongers (dealers in hides and tanning; the hides were used in parchment and vellum making), tanners and leather dressers for example. Type in a surname or place in the search box and click on the result to reveal information such as name, dates trading, location and the source of the information. The Scottish Book Trade Index is at **www.nls.uk/catalogues/ scottish-book-trade-index** and lists the trades and addresses of people involved in printing in Scotland up to 1850, including printers, publishers, booksellers, bookbinders, stationers and papermakers.

The British Association of Paper Historians (BAPH **http://baph.org.uk**) is useful, with images of paper-mills and the history of papermaking in the UK. **www.papermakers.org.uk** intends to be a genealogical base for papermakers but, at the time of writing, was a work in progress, listing some papermakers from the 1881 census from Berkshire, Hampshire and Oxfordshire.

Saddle and Harness Makers

In the days before motorcars, the horse was king. For many, no criminal was more heinous that the horse thief (calling someone this was a term of abuse) and in the Middle Ages the offence was

Horses showing off their harnesses. Postcard dated 1907. (Author's collection, ©Adèle Emm)

punishable by death. A multitude of trades and crafts were associated with the horse: coaching inn, coachbuilder, saddle and harness maker, loriner, blacksmith and horse-brass maker, to mention a few. Harness makers needed straw for padding horse collars, while saddles were filled with wool, consolidating the symbiotic relationship with the countryside.

There could be money in saddle and harness making. George Emm died in 1901 leaving £1,830 12s 6d to his son, Henry John. Not only did the saddler make the paraphernalia for the horse and carriage but, as George's great-granddaughter Nancy Cawthorne points out, George's customers included football and cricket clubs (repairing bats and balls), Paulton Hospital (leather belts to restrain patients on the operating table) and Paulton churchwardens (bell-ropes). Saddlers repaired harnesses and saddles and, like the cordwainer (see Chapter 8), occasionally skinned horses. Unfortunately, G. Emm & Son Saddle, Collar and Harness Makers didn't survive long after the Second World War and the rise of the motorcar. His archives, including ledgers and account books, are lodged with Radstock, Midsomer Norton and District Museum **http://radstockmuseum.co.uk**.

The loriner made spurs, bits and stirrups from metal. In Cheapside, London, in 1327, the saddlers and loriners came to blows over their rights to horse appurtenances. Further down the order of preference at fifty-seven, the Worshipful Company of Loriners **www.loriner.co.uk** is the oldest guild apart from the Cappers. Their ordinances date from 1261 but there are no membership records prior to 1722; the archives are held in Guildhall. Other records may be hard to locate but, as usual, try record offices.

The Worshipful Company of Saddlers **www.saddlersco.co.uk** is twenty-fifth in the order of preference. The original medieval hall built in around 1395 was destroyed in the Great Fire and the replacement hall built in 1822 was destroyed in 1940, together with the majority of their records. Surviving archives held at Saddlers' Hall are listed on **www.saddlersco.co.uk/thesaddlerscompany/ archives.html**. The Company Archivist will answer queries by email, telephone or post. Durham Saddlers' records for 1753 and 1800 are held at Durham University.

Other archives are lodged locally and surviving records could be held anywhere throughout the country. Discovery **http://discovery. nationalarchives.gov.uk** may locate some, although whether you'll find your saddler is a matter of serendipity. Typing 'saddler' brought up over 1,032 results including indentures, training agreements, draft transfers, price lists and letters from saddlers to customers.

Wheelwrights and Coachbuilders

Imagine how strong wheels had to be to carry up to a ton of weight over atrociously rutted, muddy roads, like those of Edward de Rowland in the 1100s, transporting stone for Exeter Cathedral.

William Edgar Emms in cloth cap working on a railway coach in Wolverton works, c.1905. Family rumour has it that this was Queen Victoria's Jubilee coach, but he is too old here. I believe the photo was taken to commemorate the completion of his apprenticeship. (Author's collection, ©Adèle Emm)

No one knows when or by whom the wheel was invented, although James Burgess, **https://archive.org/stream/practical treatis00burg#** suggests in his 1881 book on coach building that it was the ancient Egyptians. Solid wheels made from planks were used in Mesopotamia from 5,000 BCE and spoked wheels, which made them lighter, were built in Asia Minor from 2,000 BCE. By about 1,500 BCE, metal rims were attached, making wheels more robust. The Romans and Saxons made wheels with spokes and continuous metal rims but the technology was forgotten when the Romans left. Wheels were then made with strakes (sections) nailed

179

to the rim which, farmers believed, gave wheels a better grip. 'Tyres' were metal (see blacksmith), fixed to the wheels when hot and cooled quickly to shrink to the wood.

Different sections of the wheel were commonly made from different woods depending on the properties required; elm for the hub, oak for spokes because they needed strength and ash for the fellies (rim) for resilience and toughness. Beech, liable to warp and rot, was occasionally used because it was cheap. My grandfather, a coachbuilder, could distinguish any type of wood by looking at and feeling it. A wheelwright needed a saw and wheel pit and tools were similar to those of carpenters and joiners: spokeshaves, callipers, drawknives and a traveller to measure the circumference of the wheel, especially when making the metal tyre. The skill was working with circles and angles and ensuring wheels and carts weren't too heavy for a horse to pull.

An apprenticeship lasted between seven and ten years and each town and the occasional village had a wheelwright. Many were also wainwrights, making not only the wheels, but also wagons, carts, ploughs and hay rakes too. In rural areas, the wheelwright, like carpenters, might double as coffin maker and undertaker. In the 1871 census there were 30,811 wheelwrights working in England and Wales, dropping in 1911 to 23,785 as the impact of motor vehicles had a disastrous effect on the trade.

The first coach was built in England for the Earl of Rutland in 1555 by Walter Rippon, ten years before Dutchman William Booner presented one to Elizabeth I. This had 'doors all round... so people might feast their eyes on the beauty of the trimming or linings'. By the 1600s, coach building was an industry, certainly in London, and incurring the wrath of the Thames watermen who justifiably saw the Hackney coach, introduced in 1605, as a potential threat although roads had to be considerably better for this to be realised. The original Hackney coaches waited in their yard until they were hired, i.e. no plying for trade in the streets. In 1635, the government limited their number to fifty but by 1662, there were 400 in London each paying £5 duty and, notwithstanding, 700 by 1694. The government

The Speaker's State Coach used in Queen Elizabeth II's coronation. Designed by Daniel Marot for William III in 1698, it shows workers in the background. Postcard dated 1906. (Author's collection, ©Adèle Emm)

passed various legislations over the years on Hackney carriages, including 1831 when it was an imprisonable offence not to pay the driver! (**www.legislation.gov.uk/ukpga/Will4/1-2/22**)

In 1810, a tax was levied on vehicle sales (repealed 1825); in 1814, 23,400 four-wheeled vehicles, 27,300 two-wheeled vehicles and 18,500 tax carts paid duty to the government. That year, 3,636 vehicles were built, rising to 5,143 ten years later with a total of 76,000 wheeled vehicles paying tax to the government in 1824.

The stagecoach was effectively the public transport system from the early seventeenth century. Originally private coaches were commandeered for this trade, but were eventually made to order. They were not a comfortable means of transport. The wealthier sat inside in cramped, smelly conditions, the rutted roads meaning they were constantly thrown around and against each other. Vulnerable to the vagaries of the weather, the more impecunious sat on top or at the back, holding tight. The Stage Coaches Act of 1788 regulated the number of people riding on top to six and two at the back. During the eighteenth century, stagecoaches were susceptible to highwaymen and robbers.

As James Burgess explains, by the end of the seventeenth century, the 'Flying Coach' could cover the ground between London and Oxford in thirteen hours. There were even discussions about restricting the speed of coaches to thirty miles a day in summer and twenty-five in winter, but nothing came of this. In 1760, it could take eighteen days to travel from Edinburgh to London with part of the journey conveyed by pack horse, the state of the roads too perilous for a coach.

The Royal State Coach still used on state occasions was built in 1762 by Samuel Butler and kept in the Royal Mews at Buckingham Palace. Daniel Kirwan's 1870 book lists the cost and the trades who worked on it. The total cost was £7,528 4s 3½d, and was followed by, writes Kirwan, 'an awful row about the bill'.

The cost was:

coachmaker (including wheelwright and smith)	£1637 15 0
carver	£2500 0 0
gilder	£935 14 0
painter	£315 0 0
laceman	£737 10 7
chaser	£665 4 6
harnessmaker	£385 15 0
mercer	£202 5 10½
beltmaker	£99 6 6
milliner	£31 3 4
saddle	£10 16 6
woollendraper	£4 3 6
covermaker	£3 9 6
Total	**£7528 4 3½**

As can be seen from the cost, a wide range of skills were required to build a coach which was basically two parts; the chassis with wheels, springs and axle, shafts and traces for the horses and the body where passengers sat. The body-maker was, according to Burgess, the most skilful of all tradesmen who had to draw out the shape from the wood, taking into consideration the grain in order to make the strongest possible body before cutting and fitting the wood carefully together. With a skilled foreman and workforce, Burgess explains, everyone could work on it together and the coach fitted like a 'Chinese puzzle'. He describes in meticulous detail the work entailed in building carriage, wheels, springs and axles, including the blacksmith's role as well as the paintwork with family crests, linings, trimmings and curtains. In the early days, coaches were built to order but, by 1881, they were ready made, much like a car today, and personalised with colour and trimmings. In effect, coachbuilders now had to build speculatively, paying in advance for everything hoping coaches would sell. Competition in the 1880s meant profit margins were extremely tight. In 1851, 16,590 men described themselves as coachmakers, rising to 23,034 by 1871. By 1874, the number of carriages on the road had increased to 482,600 with 125,000 paying duty to the government.

The introduction of the railways from the 1830s terminated the age of the stagecoach. A coachbuilder had to diversify into other horse-drawn vehicles such as phaetons, railway carriages and eventually motor vehicles. Unfortunately, many companies producing horse-drawn vehicles failed to negotiate the change.

Coinciding with the emergence of the railways, the first omnibus in London was launched in 1829 by George Shillibeer, who'd seen similar enterprises while working as a coachbuilder in Paris. Initially carrying twenty-two people inside a coach pulled by three horses, its route was from the Yorkshire Stingo pub in Paddington to Bank. The fare? A shilling. By 1881, the London General Omnibus Company ran about 628 buses with 6,935 horses travelling six miles a day at an average of six miles an hour. The buses were built and maintained by their own workforce.

One company which successfully negotiated the death of the coach and the development of the horseless carriage was Salmons of Newport Pagnell. Founded around 1830 by Joseph Salmons (1796–1878) in Tickford Street, hence Tickford Motors, this company made coaches, dog-carts and ralli-carts sold around the world and was among the earliest coachbuilders to build motor carriages from 1898. The census records from 1841 are full of men classing themselves as coachbuilders or journeymen coachbuilders and invariably they were working at Salmons. Joseph's first job was wheelwright and the excellent book *Salmons and Sons* by Dennis Mynard explains the history of this fascinating company, the workers, the prices paid for coaches, carts and eventually cars and much of Newport Pagnell's history to 1955 when the firm was bought by David Brown of Aston Martin fame. If you have ancestors in Newport Pagnell and surrounding districts, you may find them mentioned in the book.

Obviously, London had more than its fair share of coach building firms, including Hoopers of Westminster (1805–1959) who supplied high quality horse-drawn carriages to royalty, among others, and were incorporated into Daimler in 1940. The City of Westminster Archives has some records but genealogical information is limited. Another firm was Thrupp and Maberly originally established near Worcester in the 1740s but moving to the Grosvenor Square area in the 1760s. Maberly joined them in the 1850s. Pick Motor Company, founded by John Pick, originally a blacksmith, operated in Stamford, Lincolnshire, from 1899 to 1925. Another Stamford firm was Henry Hayes and Son, in business from 1825 to 1924. Unfortunately, even though in the 1871 census twenty-nine men and seven boys were employed, no records have survived.

Hints as to where coachmakers and builders worked can be found in pub names. Coach building families Duffet (1871 census) and Deacon (1881 census) were licensees at the Coachmakers Arms in Southsea.

The Worshipful Company of Coachmakers and Coach Harness Makers **http://coachmakers.co.uk** received its Charter from

Charles II in 1677 and its rules ensured that no one could execute the trade of coach or coach harness maker within twenty miles of London without belonging to the Company. Unfortunately, most records were destroyed in the Second World War, although the 1761 model for the Royal State Coach and other treasures had been removed beforehand. Guildhall has details of any archives still in existence.

Other coach building companies and coach design development in London are explained in the useful **www.british-history.ac.uk/report.aspx?compid=22174**. The National Motor Museum in Beaulieu **www.nationalmotormuseum.org.uk** may be of interest, as might the various publications heralding the industry such as *The Coach Builders', Harness makers' and Saddlers' Art Journal*, published from 1880, some copies of which are held at the museum in its extensive reference library on the motor and coach industry. Access is by appointment. It is unlikely you will find any genealogical information. Your best bet, as usual, is to search relevant record offices. Some forums exist with information on coachbuilders, although many are twentieth century.

Places to Visit

This is not an exhaustive list.

• Coventry Transport Museum, Coventry **www.transport-museum.com**
• Haynes Motor Museum, Sparkford, Yeovil, Somerset **www.haynesmotormuseum.com**
• Heritage Motor Centre, Gaydon, Warwickshire **www.heritage-motor-centre.co.uk**
• John Jarrold Printing Museum, Norwich **www.johnjarroldprintingmuseum.org.uk**; bookbinding demonstrations
• Museum of Leathercraft, Abington Museum, Abington Park, Northampton. **www.museumofleathercraft.org**; saddles, clothing and bookbinding etc.

• Leather Museum, Walsall, **http://cms.walsall.gov.uk/
leathermuseum**; workshops on leather goods making and an
exhibition of royal saddles.

• London Transport Museum **www.ltmuseum.co.uk**

• National Motor Museum at Beaulieu **www.nationalmotor
museum.org.uk** large collection of not just cars, but also a
charitable trust dedicated to preserving and promoting motoring
history.

• Museum of Science and Industry Manchester **www.mosi.org.uk**

• Science Museum **www.sciencemuseum.org.uk**

Chapter 11
OTHER GENEALOGICAL RESOURCES

Genealogy Sites

Subscription services

There are plenty of subscription sites, each specialising in different areas. The most useful for genealogists are **www.ancestry.co.uk** and **www.findmypast.co.uk**, both with frequently updated information, so check frequently for what's new. Collections depend on which subscription service you use. Both have directories such as *Pigot's* and electoral registers. The Genealogist **www.thegenealogist.co.uk** has tithe records plus some transcriptions of parish registers and is good for Nonconformist sources.

Origins **www.origins.net** is useful for London research, London apprentice abstracts and wills pre-1858 but, by the time of publication, may be subsumed into FindMyPast. Other genealogical sites include **www.parishchest.com**, **www.parishregister.com**, **www.genesreunited.co.uk**, **www.deceasedonline.com** and **www.myheritage.com**. The SoG and many libraries subscribe to many sites, giving free access.

Free services

Free genealogical sites are **www.freebmd.org.uk** and its sister site **www.freecen.org.uk**, aiming to give access to the 1841–91 censuses; **www.ukbmd.org.uk** offers locally created indexes for birth, marriage and death as well as access to Online Parish Clerks **www.ukbmd.org.uk/online_parish_clerk** and **www.freereg.org.uk** with indexes and transcriptions of parish registers. The Society of Genealogists is at **www.sog.org.uk** (although you must be a member to use some online services) and **http://forebears.co.uk** is a good portal for other sites. Don't forget Family Search at **https:// familysearch.org/search/collection/igi**.

Through collaboration between the Open University and the Universities of Hertfordshire and Bedfordshire and funded by the Arts and Humanities Research Council, **www.oldbaileyonline.org** is a fully searchable free database for all trials held at London Central Criminal Courts from 1674 to 1913. Be aware that, although trials were held in London, people gravitated to the capital, such as former button maker, Elias Smith from Ludlow, condemned for horse stealing in 1686.

You must register for the free forum to post genealogical questions at British Genealogy **www.british-genealogy.com**. Rootsweb occupations mailing list is at **www.rootsweb. ancestry. com/~jfuller/gen_mail_occ.html**. There is a timeline of dates and resources, such as Ecclesiastical and Assize Courts, compiled by genealogist Roy Stockdill, at **www.british-genealogy.com/ resources-and-guides/seminal-dates.php**.

Online Historical Population Reports (OHPR)

www.histpop.org, based at Essex University, has online access to the census reports (not enumerators' books) for Britain and Ireland from 1801 to 1937. It is an in-depth view of the economy and society of the nineteenth and early twentieth centuries and has a breakdown of the numbers of people working in different occupations from the 1831 censuses onwards. Although of no biographical use, this site has useful links to all genealogical databases, both subscription and free.

Genuki

www.genuki.org.uk is another useful free search engine e.g. search 'goldsmiths' and find sources throughout the country. It gives addresses and contact details for county record offices.

The National Archives and Discovery (formerly A2A)

Ruskin Avenue, Kew, Richmond, Surrey, TW9 4DU. Tel: 020 8876 3444, **www.nationalarchives.gov.uk** and **http://discovery.national archives.gov.uk**.

In 2014, with hopes for completion by 2016, A2A morphed into Discovery to access all possible archives from one portal and identify all sources into one integrated catalogue. Guides to the Poor Law can be found on **www.nationalarchives.gov.uk/records/research-guides/poor-laws.htm** with a link to a recommended book list for finding countywide records. Their research guides are particularly helpful and can be found online. The London Family History Centre run by the Church of the Latter Day Saints (Mormons) is, at the time of writing, based at the National Archives but looking for a new home.

The National Archives of Northern Ireland

2 Titanic Boulevard, Belfast, BT3 9HQ. Tel: 0289 053 4800, **www. proni.gov.uk**, email: proni@dcalni.gov.uk.

National Archives of Scotland

2 Princes Street, Edinburgh, EH1 3YY. Tel: 0131 535 1314, **www. nas.gov.uk**, email: enquiries@nas.gov.uk.

British History – see also Victoria County Histories

www.british-history.ac.uk is a valuable website run by the University of London and the History of Parliament Trust. It can be searched by region, name, urban and metropolitan districts and is a fascinating view into archives and records. A huge amount is free but not all and, at the time of writing, subscription was a reasonable £30 per annum. The University of London's **www.history.ac.uk** is involved in the Rollco Project (see Chapter 2) and the history of London and other cities. The BBC gives a flavour to Victorian middle class, society and industry at **www.bbc.co.uk/history/british/victorians**.

Cyndislist

Free **www.cyndislist.com/uk** is a world wide database and may be useful if your ancestors migrated.

Directories

Some *Kelly's* (after Frederic Festus Kelly, d.1883), *Pigot's*, Post Office and telephone directories have been digitised (FindMyPast and Ancestry). Your library and record office may have local directories which are, of course, viewable for free. Check what is available before visiting. The University of Leicester has digitised some directories, found free online at **http://specialcollections.le.ac.uk/cdm/landingpage/collection/p16445coll4** (formerly **www.historicaldirectories.org**) and these include, for instance: *Kelly's Directory* for Staffordshire 1896; the *Post Office Directory* for Birmingham, Staffordshire and Worcester 1850, and *Peck's Trade Directories of Birmingham* 1896–97. The originals are in Birmingham Central Library. Be aware that directories have flaws; not everybody is listed (you paid to be in them, so were therefore financially secure enough to do so) and there may be mistakes insofar as they were not always updated. It is estimated that only six percent of London's residents from the 1851 census are listed in London's Post Office directories, usually the wealthier ones.

Museums of Rural Life

At Reading University **www.reading.ac.uk/merl**, the Museum of English Rural Life has collections and archives relating to agriculture and the rural economy. The National Museum of Rural Life, Scotland **www.nms.ac.uk/our_museums/museum_of_rural_life.aspx** has a supply of photographs on the Scottish Life Archive section **www.nms.ac.uk/explore/collections-stories/scottish-history-and -archaeology/scottish-life-archive**.

Films

It is incredibly unlikely you will find a film of an ancestor unless they are famous, but old films are a fascinating glimpse into the past. Many can be accessed online although, should you wish to download a copy, you usually pay. Pathé News, **www.british pathe.com**, whose archive is based on thrice-weekly newsreels projected at cinemas, has over 90,000 clips dating from the beginning of the twentieth century to 1970. The North West Film Archive **www.nwfa.mmu.ac.uk**, run by Manchester Metropolitan University Library's Special Collections based at Manchester's Central Library, has films of industry, work and home life of communities in North West England from the 1890s to today. By putting in a keyword on their search facility e.g. blacksmith, you can view scenes such as Irlam steelworks dated 1935, iron clog making from 1945 and Soutergate blacksmith John Coward shoeing a horse in 1946. In this case, the blacksmith is named. The BBC and ITN also have online archives often viewed for free at **www.gettyimages.co.uk** and **www.itnsource.com/en**.

Society of Genealogists' Library

14 Charterhouse Buildings, Goswell Road, London, EC1M 7BA. Tel: 020 7251 8799 – closed Sunday, Monday and Friday. Free for members, a daily rate for others. **www.sog.org.uk**, email: librarian@sog.org.uk.

Grace's Guide

This wiki **www.gracesguide.co.uk** provides historical information on manufacturing in Britain. Key your industry into the search box for information on various manufacturing companies. Additions are added daily.

Guildhall Library

Aldermanbury, London, EC2V 7HH. Tel: 020 7332 1868, email:

guildhall.library@cityoflondon.gov.uk. **www.cityoflondon.gov.uk/
things-to-do/visiting-the-city/archives-and-city-history/guildhall
-library/Pages/default.aspx**

www.history.ac.uk/gh/18v.htm lists all the almshouse records
available at Guildhall including: bakers, brewers, coopers,
fishmongers, fishmongers and poulterers, grocers and haberdashers.
See British History above.

Hearth tax

Run and maintained by Roehampton University's Centre for Hearth
Tax Research, this free site **www.hearthtax.org.uk** gives basic
information (surname, where they live and whether the person pays)
for the tax introduced in England and Wales in 1662 during the reign
of Charles II. Not all counties have been transcribed and the project
is releasing information as they research it. Many records are in poor
condition due to damp and deterioration of the ink. This particular
tax was unpopular as it involved an inspection of all homes. Those
too poor to pay poor rates or who owned property worth less than
twenty shillings a year were exempt. The issue here is whether your
family could afford or were too impoverished to pay taxes. The
records are held at the National Archives in E179 with an
explanation of taxation prior to 1689 on **www.national
archives.gov.uk/records/research-guides/taxation-before-1689
.htm**.

London Metropolitan Archives

40 Northampton Road, London, EC1R OHB. Tel: 020 7332 3820.
Email ask.lma@cityoflondon.gov.uk. **www.cityoflondon.gov.uk/lma**,
online catalogue at **http://search.lma.gov.uk/opac_lma/index.
htm**.

You need a free history card to use the online search facility at
LMA and to access original documents at the centre itself. Many
records are digitised and can be accessed through **www.ancestry.**

co.uk. The LMA computers have free access to Ancestry, digitised copies of *The Times*, *The Daily Mirror* and seventeenth to nineteenth century British Library Collections, plus other sources. It has excellent free information leaflets found online and in the centre covering a range of London research including:

- Searching for members or those apprenticed to members of City of London Companies
- City Freedom Archives
- Membership records of the Merchant Taylors' Company
- Licensed Victuallers' Records
- Directories of London and the Home Counties
- George Goodwin and *The Builder*

London Lives

Sessions Papers and Middlesex Justices' records have been digitised free to view on **www.londonlives.org**. There are over 3.35 million names including some biographies. Fully searchable, it provides a fascinating mirror of crime, poverty and social policy in London. By typing in 'goldsmith', Middlesex sessions papers (among others) appear and you can read the transcript and look via a magnifier at the original page. It is possible to search a name but with variable results. **http://spitalfieldslife.com** is a contemporary blog with historical photos and adverts. Old Bailey Online **www.oldbailey online.org** is a free site for the Central Criminal Court.

Maps

Enclosure maps are useful from roughly 1800 as they are large scale. Local libraries and record offices hold them together with older and more specialised maps of varied dates and scale. The Charles Close Society www.charlesclosesociety.org, founded by Ordnance Survey enthusiasts in 1980, has a useful online map-finding service giving advice on locating old maps. Key in the relevant address on **www.**

charlesclosesociety.org/CCS-sheetfinder and see what is available.

It is possible to buy map reproductions; I bought one dated 1848 for 50p in a sale at my local library. Second-hand bookshops, charity shops, specialist shops and bookshops at museums sell them and some can be bought online from commercial companies such as **www.alangodfreymaps.co.uk**, **www.mapseeker.co.uk**, **www.past pages.co.uk**, and **www.old-maps.co.uk/index.html**. By double-clicking on a map of the UK, it shows what map, scale and dates are available and at what cost. Some archive maps are online, although many are too small to see detail. Lee Jackson's website **www. victorianlondon.org** has some maps of London. The National Library of Scotland has a variety of maps from the Reform Act of 1832 found online at **http://maps.nls.uk**. An 1866–67 map of Aberdeen, for instance, is on **http://maps.nls.uk/townplans/ aberdeen.html**. Maps can be enlarged and printed from your home computer.

Charles Booth's maps showing the poverty of London street by street is a fascinating if ghoulish reminder of London's poverty and found online at **http://booth.lse.ac.uk**. The SoG has copies of the original books. The earliest 1889 Booth maps can be found online via the University of Michigan at **www.umich.edu/~risotto**.

For the definitive map experience, you must go to the British Library map room **www.bl.uk/reshelp/bldept/maps**. No maps can be removed from the library. A reader's ticket (free) is essential.

Newspapers, Magazines and Books

The first daily newspaper in England was *The Daily Courant* (1702–35). Consisting of one sheet, it had news on the front and advertisements on the reverse. A history of newspapers, regulation and taxes **www.newspapersoc.org.uk/history-of-british-news papers** is on the Newspaper Society **www.newspapersoc. org.uk** website.

The British Library's superlative British Newspaper Archive, dating mainly from the nineteenth century, is currently being digitised. Newspapers already microfilmed and digitised can be viewed for free with a reader's ticket in the St Pancras and Boston Spa reading rooms. Print copies of magazines held in Yorkshire can be viewed in the St Pancras reading rooms if ordered up forty-eight hours in advance and in a good enough condition to travel. See the website for details **www.bl.uk**.

Microfilms of local and regional newspapers (e.g. *The Bucks Standard* and *The Manchester Evening News*) are held at central libraries and record offices. If you know your ancestors traded in a certain town or village, look for them in the relevant papers but be prepared to scan through a lot of pages. FindMyPast has an online local British newspaper collection 1710–1953.

Several newspapers such as *The Scotsman* **http://archive. scotsman.com**, *The Times* **www.thetimes.co.uk/tto/archive** and *The Guardian/Observer* **http://pqasb.pqarchiver.com/guardian/ advancedsearch.html** have subscription online archives, accessible for free if your library has a subscription. Another subscription service is **www.britishnewspaperarchive.co.uk** and, again, your library may subscribe.

The *London Gazette* **www.thegazette.co.uk** has been published every weekday except Bank Holidays since 1665 and is an official public record of the British government. It is useful for bankruptcies, insolvencies, patents applications, appointments to public office and changes of name. There are *Gazettes* for Edinburgh, first published 1699, and Belfast from 1921.

Several occupations have their own trade magazines, such as *Licensed Victuallers Guardian* 1869–87, but genealogical information may be minimal.

Some commercial companies such as **www.tilleys vintage magazines.com** and Ken's Paper Collectibles **www.kens. co.uk** in Newport Pagnell sell original vintage magazines and other paper ephemera. The Ephemera Society might be useful **www. ephemera-society.org.uk** as well as **http://ephemera.ning.com/group/ ephemeradealers** and **www.pastpages.co.uk**. Alternatively, search for vintage shops and postcard fairs online. As they sell what they have in stock, dealers may not have what you want.

For books, Amazon is useful as is **http://books.google.com**. The Gutenberg Project **www.gutenberg.org** and **https://archive. org/details/texts** have digitised some out-of-copyright books. Bizarrely, you may find British information in other countries' national libraries and universities, such as the National Library of Australia **http://trove.nla.gov.au**.

Photographs

The earliest recognisable photographs are William Henry Fox Talbot's (1800–77) calotypes from the 1840s. However, in effect most are dated after the (rare) 1850s and more commonly from the 1860s. The Museum of English Rural Life has over 750,000 photographs, although you are unlikely to recognise an ancestor; most 'sitters' are unidentified. Photographs are catalogued by location, as is the extensive Francis Frith (1822–98) **www.francisfrith.com** archive, published in coffee-table style books. This site is useful for maps and books of the area. Local, county and specialist libraries have photo archives. Again, your ancestor may be named, but usually people appearing in general scenes are not recorded. Your best bet, once you know the area where your ancestors lived, is to contact the local library, family history association and county libraries and search through their records. Many libraries' photo collections are online.

Postcard fairs are an unusual source and cards showing occupations can be pricy – up to £50 is not uncommon. Postcards of the town or village from which your ancestors originated are a pleasant trophy of a bygone age. Postcard heyday was roughly 1900 to the beginning of the First World War. Getty Images (see film) has a stills archive.

Poor Law and Settlement

Settlement examinations from the various Poor Law Acts, which started in 1601, give information on place of birth, apprenticeships served and employment history. The SoG has extensive records. Poor Law records before 1834 are parish based and kept locally; the Archon Directory **www.nationalarchives.gov.uk/archon** might help locate them. The *Poor Law Union Gazette* carried adverts for missing mothers and some editions are held at the British Library newspaper collection and via subscription at the British Newspaper Archive. **www.genguide.co.uk/source/workhouse-records-poor-law-unions/53** explains workhouse records, as does the National Archives website.

The Victoria and Albert Museum

The museum has some interesting articles online to give background to trade and industry. For example, **www.vam.ac.uk/content/articles/s/industry-power-and-social-change** and **www.vam.ac.uk/page/i/industrial-revolution**.

Victoria County History

This enterprise, originally started in 1898, resulted in the famous large red volumes found in virtually every record office and many libraries. There are fourteen county sets for most counties apart from Northumberland and the West Riding of Yorkshire. Paperback copies can be bought online from **www.victoriacountyhistory.ac.uk** and, although they give little information on crafts, you may find the local squire or important businessman referenced here. As part of the Institute of Historical Research based at London University, also responsible for British History Online, they conceived the England's Past for Everyone (EPE) project **www.victoriacountyhistory.ac.uk/publications-projects/epe** which has led to the publication of books such as Simon Townley's *Henley on Thames, Town, Trade and River*. Few, however, are dedicated closely to trade.

Victorian London

Lee Jackson's dictionary is on **www.victorianlondon.org**.

SELECT BIBLIOGRAPHY
AND FURTHER READING

As family history research is such a popular hobby, there are hundreds of books available, both general and more specific. This is not an exhaustive list.

The Book of Trades or Library of Useful Arts 1806, found online via Google books
The Book of Trades or Library of Useful Arts 1818 **https://archive. org/stream/bookenglishtrad00soutgoog#page/n9/mode/2up**
Cunningham, Peter *Handbook of London*, John Murray, 1850 **https://archive.org/stream/handbookoflondon00cunn**
Kirwan, Daniel Joseph *Palace and Hovel or Phases of London Life*, Hartford, Belnap & Bliss 1870 **https://archive.org/details/ palacehovel00kirw**, description of London by an 1870s American tourist
Inglis, Lucy *Georgian London, Into the Streets*. Her blog **http:// georgianlondon.com** and **http://lucyinglis.tumblr.com** has articles on artisan and immigrant communities from 1660 to 1830; limited genealogical information
Mayhew, Henry *London labour and the London Poor*, published in serial form from1840s, Wordsworth, 2008
Online Historical Population Reports (OHPR) **www.histpop.org**, breakdowns of occupations from 1831
Taxation before 1689 explanation and sources at the National Archives **www.nationalarchives.gov.uk/records/research-guides/taxation-before-1689.htm** Includes links to palaeography tutorials
www.victorianweb.org/history/census.html occupations breakdown 1851–71

Chapter 1
Barratt, Nick *Who do you think you are? Encyclopedia of Genealogy*, Harper Collins, 2008
Christian, Peter *The Genealogist's Internet*, Bloomsbury, 2012
Clifford, David, J.H. *My Ancestors were Congregationalists*, Society of Genealogists, 1998

Fowler, Simon *Poor Law Records for Family Historians*, Family History Partnership, 2011

Gandy, Michael *Tracing Nonconformist Ancestors*, PRO, 2001

Gibson, Jeremy; Hampson, Elizabeth; Raymond, Stuart *Marriage Indexes for Family Historians*, Family History Partnership, 2008

Grannum, Karen; Taylor, Nigel *Wills and Probate Records*, National Archives, 2009

Heywood, Thomas *If You Know Not Me, You Know Nobody* Part 2, play about the life of haberdashery apprentices and the founding of the Royal Exchange, London,1605–06

McKie, David *What's in a Surname? A Journey from Abercrombie to Zwicker*, Random House, 2013

Mortimer, Ian *The Time Travellers' Guide to Medieval England*, Vintage, 2009, offers background and living conditions to, among others, guilds, wool industries, fishmongers, merchants and mercers. See also *The Time Travellers' Guide to Elizabethan England*, 2013.

Paton, Chris *Tracing Your Family History on the Internet*, Pen and Sword, 2014

Raymond, Stuart A. *Trades and Professions*, Family History Partnership, 2011

Raymond, Stuart A. *The Wills of our Ancestors*, Pen and Sword, 2012

Chapter 2

City of London Livery Companies and Related Organisations, A Guide to their Archives in Guildhall Library 4th ed., 2010

The Guide to Greater London History Sources Volume 1, *The City of London.*

Leighton, W.A. *The Guilds of Shrewsbury*, 1881

Melling, John Kennedy *London Guilds and Liveries*, Shire, 2008

Selles, Maud (Ed.) *The York Mercers and Merchant Adventurers 1356–1917*, Andrews, 1918 **https://archive.org/details/york mercersmerch00 mercrich**

Chapter 3

Crail, Mark *Tracing your Labour Movement Ancestors*, Pen and Sword, 2009

Dennis, Victoria Solt *Discovering Friendly and Fraternal Societies, Their Badges and Regalia*, Shire, 2005

Devon County Council **www.devon.gov.uk/apprenticeship_ records** description of apprenticeships, links to locating records and further reading

Harwood, Jeremy *Holidays and Hard Times 1870s*, Reader's Digest, 2009

Kay, J.A.; Morris, C.N.; Jaffer, S.M.; Meadowcroft, S.A. *The Regulation of Retail Trading Hours*, The Institute for Fiscal Studies, 1984, **www.ifs.org.uk/comms/r13.pdf**, economic background to retailing before 1839

Loman, Roger *An Introduction to Friendly Society Records*, Federation of Family History Societies, 2000

Moffrey, Robert W. *The Rise and Progress of the Manchester Unity of the Independent Order of Oddfellows, 1810–1904* online at **www.isle-of-man.com/manxnotebook/history/socs/odf_ mdly.htm**, 1904

Morley, Shaun (Ed.) *Oxfordshire Friendly Societies, 1750–1918*, Oxfordshire Record Society, Volume 68, 2011

Parliament and the history of UK legislation **www.parliament.uk/about/living-heritage/transformingsociety** pivotal Acts of Parliament. Also **www.portcullis.parliament.uk** and **www.parliament.uk/ archives**. **www.legislation.gov.uk** is the official home of enacted UK legislation 1267 to present

Raymond, Stuart *My Ancestor was an Apprentice*, Society of Genealogists, 2010

Weinbren, Daniel *The Oddfellows, 1810–2010, 200 Years of Making Friends and Helping People*, Carnegie, 2010

Wigley, John *The Rise and Fall of the Victorian Sunday*, Manchester University, 1980

Chapter 4

Baxter, Ian A. *Baxter's Guide, Biographical Sources in the East India Office*, 3rd ed, Families in British India Society, 2004

The Grocer 1862 onwards; prices of foodstuffs together, reports of bankrupts, small ads for wide variety of companies not just grocers

Coal Merchants

Brown, R.S. *Digging for History in the Coal Merchants' Archives: the history of the Society of Coal Merchants*, Society of Coal Merchants, 1988

Edington, Robert *A Treatise on the Coal Trade*, London, 1813, explains charters, taxes and cost of shipping. Online at several sites including **http://babel.hathitrust.org/cgi/pt?id=umn.319510017749806;view=1up;seq=1.**

Elliott, Brian *Tracing your Coal Mining Ancestors*, Pen and Sword, 2014

Nef, J.U. *The Rise of the British Coal Industry Vol 1 and 2*, Routledge, 1932

Simon Grant-Jones, blacksmith **www.simongrant-jones.com**

Coffee, Chocolate and Tea Merchants
Masset, Claire *Tea and Tea Drinking*, Shire, 2010
UK Tea Council **www.tea.co.uk**. East India Company, tea trade, smuggling, history of adding milk etc.
UK Tea & Infusions Association (UKTIA) **www.tea.co.uk**

Mercers
Jefferson, Lisa *Medieval Accounts Books of the Mercers of London, An Edition and Translation*, Ashgate 2008

Tobacconists and Tobacco
Tobacco timeline **http://archive.tobacco.org/History/Tobacco_history.html**
Apperson, G.L. *The Social History of Smoking*, London, 1914 **www.gutenberg.org/files/18096/18096-h/18096-h.htm**
Cessford, Craig *The Archaeology of the Clay Pipe and the Study of Smoking*, 2001, issue 6 Assemblage **www.assemblage.group.shef.ac.uk/issue6/Cessford_text_web.htm**
Edwards, Lloyd J. *Tyneside Tobacco Pipe Makers and Tobacconists in Newcastle and Gateshead until c.1800*, **etheses.dur.ac.uk/6882/1/6882_4187**, Durham University, 1986

Victuallers/Vintners
Charleton, Walter *The Vintner's Mystery Display'd, Or The Whole Art of the Wine Trade Laid Open*, circa 1700–05
Fowler, Simon *Researching Brewery and Publican Ancestors*, Family History Partnership, 2009
Gibson Jeremy; Hunter Judith *Victuallers' Licences, Records for Family and Local Historians*, Family History Partnership, 2009
Hurst, Donald; Mynard, Dennis *One More for the Road, The history of Newport Pagnell's Inns and Public Houses*, Newport Pagnell Historical Society, 1999

Chapter 5
Ackermann *The Repository of Arts, Literature, Commerce, Manufacturers, Fashions and Politics*, London, 1809–1829 online via Google books and **Archive.org**.
Horn, Pamela *Behind the Counter; shop lives from market stall to supermarket*, Sutton, 2006

Masset, Claire *Department Stores*, Shire, 2010

Mawer, Brian *Sugar Bakers, from Sweat to Sweetness*, AGFHS, 2011; database and website of Sugar Bakers and Sugar Refiners at **www.mawer.clara.net/intro.html**

O'Day, Rosemary *The Routledge Companion to the Tudor Age*, Routledge, 2010

Smith, Colin Stephen *The Market Place and the Market's Place in London c1660–1840*, PhD thesis University College London, 1999 **http://discovery.ucl.ac.uk/1318007/1/313021.pdf**

Whitbourn, Frank *Mr Lock of St James's Street, his Continuing Life and Changing Times,*1971

White, Jerry *London in the Eighteenth Century, A Great and Monstrous Thing*, Bodley Head, 2012

Wilkinson, Philip *Turn Back Time, The High Street*, Quercus, 2010

Winstanley, Michael (Ed.) *A Traditional Grocer, T.D Smith's of Lancaster, 1858–1981*, Centre for North West Regional Studies, 1991

Winstanley, Michael J. *The Shopkeeper's World 1830–1914*, Manchester University, 1983

Chapter 6
Auctioneers

Chapman, D.H. *The Chartered Auctioneers' and Estate Agents' Institute, A Short History*, London, 1970

Bricklayers and Brickmaking

Brick Directory history of bricks **www.brickdirectory.co.uk/html/brick_history.html**

British Brick Society **http://britishbricksoc.co.uk**

Painters

Baty, Patrick *A history of the house painting trade in London ca.1660–1850* **www.scribd.com/doc/11355977/A-history-of-the- house-painting-trade-in-London-ca16601850**

Salaman, R.A. *Dictionary of tools used in the woodworking and allied trades c1700–1970*, George Allen, 1975

Chapter 7
Blacksmiths

McDougall, David, L. *The Country Blacksmith*, Shire, 2013

Goldsmiths and Silversmiths

Grimwade, Arthur G. *London Goldsmiths 1697–1837*, Faber and Faber 1976 has hallmarks and dates including biographical dictionary

Jefferson, Lisa (Ed.) *Wardens' Accounts and Court Minute Books of the Goldsmiths' Mistery of London 1334–1446*, Boydell, 2003

Reddaway T.F.; Walker, Lorna E.M. *The Early History of the Goldsmiths' Company 1327–1509,* Edward Arnold, 1975

Jewellers and Watch/Clockmakers

Baillie, G.H. *Watchmakers and Clockmakers of the World*, Mowbray, 1947, also on Ancestry

Clutton, Cecil; Baillie, G.H.; Ilbert, C.A. (Eds) *Britten's Old Clocks and Watches and Their Makers*, Methuen 1894 & 1899, republished 1982

Saunier, Claudius *Watchmaker's Handbook*, Tripplin, London, 1881 online at **https://archive.org/stream/watchmakershand 00tripgoog**

Sobel, Dava *Longitude*, Harper Perennial, 2005, novel about quest and solution for calculating longitude

Chapter 8

Magazines such as *Shoe and Leather News*, *Boot and Shoe Trade Journals* and *St Crispin*

Anon, *Toilers in London; or Inquiries concerning Female Labour in the Metropolis*, Chapter 23, Boot and Shoe Makers, 1889 **www.victorian london.org/publications3/newtoilers-23.htm**

Historical Survey of Shoe Making, British United Shoe Machinery Co. Ltd, Union Works, Leicester, 1932

Blair, John; Ramsey, Nigel (Eds), *English Medieval Industries*, Hambledon, 1991 chapter by John Cherry on leather working including tanning, curriers, making leather bottles, buckets, saddles, gloves etc.

Brown, Cynthia *Northampton 1835–1985, Shoe town, New Town*, Phillimore/Northampton Borough Council, 1990

Clarks shoes **www.clarks.co.uk** information on their history

Doyle, Arthur Conan *The Debatable Case of Mrs. Emsley*, Walter Emm's murder trial **http://gutenbergnet/au/ebooks06/ 060441h.html**

Dr Martens history **http://uk.drmartens.com/uk/history**

Holmes, Ken *Two Centuries of Shoemaking: Start-rite, 1792–1992*, 1992

Ledger, Florence E. *Put Your Foot Down, A Treatise on the History of Shoes*, Uffington, 1985

Liberty Shoe factory, Leicester University; **www.le.ac.uk/ manufacturingpasts**

Riello, Giorgio; McNeil, Peter (Eds) *Shoes, A History from Sandals to Sneakers*, Berg, 2006

Sparks, W.L. *Shoemaking in Norwich*, National Institute of the Boot and Shoe Industry, 1949

Sutton, George Barry *C & J Clark, 1833–1903, A History of Shoemaking in Street, Somerset*, William Sessions 1979

Swann, June *Shoemaking*, Shire, 1986

Virtual Shoe Museum **www.virtualshoemuseum.com**

Miscellanea

Bata-ville: We Are Not Afraid of the Future, documentary written and directed by Karen Guthrie & Nina Pope **www.bata-ville.com**

Bates, H.E. *The Feast of July*, novel including references to small shoemaking factories in 1890s Northampton

Bates, H.E. *The Vanished World*, autobiography including 1890s footwear factories

Brighouse, Harold *Hobson's Choice*, 1916, play about a Salford shoemaker and his daughters

Kinky Boots, film about Northampton shoemaking, director Julian Jarrold, 2005

Chapter 9

Burnette, Joyce *Gender, Work and Wages in Industrial Revolution Britain*, Cambridge University, 2011

Davies, Clarice Stella (Ed.) *A History of Macclesfield*, University of Manchester, 1961

Waggett, Ralph W. *A History of the Worshipful Company of Glovers of London*, Phillimore, 2000

Tailors and Seamstresses

Mayhew, Henry *Letter VI*, harrowing description of 1849–50 sweatshops and slopshops **www.victorianlondon.org/ professions/sloptrade.htm**

Glovers

Beck, William *Gloves, Their Annals and Associations*, Hamilton, Adams, 1883 **https://archive.org/stream/glovestheiranna00 unkngoog#page/n5/mode/2up**

Dent, Allcroft and Co. and other glove companies **www.gracesguide. co.uk**

Waggett, Ralph *A History of the Worshipful Company of Glovers of London*, Phillimore 2nd Ed, 2007

Wood, Mrs Henry *Mrs Halliburton's Troubles*, London, 1862 explanation of glove trade including their manufacture. **www.gutenberg.org/ebooks/34587** or **https://archive.org/details/mrshalliburtonst00wood_0**

Hat Making

Christys Hats **www.christys-hats.com**

Hertfordshire Genealogy, straw hat information **http://www.hertfordshire-genealogy.co.uk/data/occupations/straw-plait.htm**

Stockport Heritage Magazine articles on Stockport hatting industry. Index on CD. Back issues and CD bought via **www.stockportheritagemagazine.co.uk**

Bunker, Stephen; Holgate, Robin; Nichols, Marian *The Changing Face of Luton*, Book Castle, 1993

Inwards, Harry, *Straw Hats, their History and Manufacture*, Pitman, 1922, republished Hard Press Publishing. Online **http://images.library.wisc.edu/HumanEcol/EFacs/MillineryBooks/MBInwardsStraw/reference/humanecol.mbinwardsstraw.i0009. pdf**

Jones, Diana *Hats Off! The story of George Carter and Sons*, BPR, 2008

McKnight, Penny *Stockport Hatting*, Stockport Metropolitan Borough Council, 2000.

Nevell, Michael; Grimsditch, Brian; Hradil, Ivan *Denton and the archaeology of the Felt Hatting Industry*, Volume 7 Archaeology of Tameside series, Tameside Metropolitan Borough Council, 2007

Reeve, Amy J. *Practical Home Millinery*, Longmans, Green & Co., 1903

Lace making

Browne, Clare *Lace from the Victoria and Albert Museum*, V&A, 2004

Channer, Catherine C.; Roberts, M.E. *Lace Making in the Midlands Past and Present*, 1900

Goldenberg, Samuel L. *Lace, its Origin and History*, 1904 via Project Gutenberg

Gray, Kirsty *Tracing your West Country Ancestors*, Pen and Sword, 2013, Chapter 7.

The Lace Guild; information on lacemaking and history in Stourbridge **www.laceguild.org www.bbc.co.uk/legacies/work/england/nottingham**; lace making in Nottingham

Newport Pagnell Historic Town Assessment Report, English Heritage, September 2010 www.buckscc.gov.uk/media/130580/newport_pagnell_consultation_report.pdf
Industrial Museum, Wollaton Hall, Nottingham Industrial Museum www.nottinghamindustrialmuseum.co.uk, lace making machines

Button Making
Dorset Button Makers www.thedorsetpage.com/history/Button_Making/button_making.htm
Hammond Turner & Sons http://hammond-turner.com/
Johns, Thelma *Dorset Buttons, Hand stitched in Dorset for over 300 Years*, Natula, 2012
Peacock, Primrose *Discovering Old Buttons*, Shire, 2008

Chapter 10
Felix, Paul; Siân Ellis; Quinn, Tom *The Book of Forgotten Crafts*, David and Charles, 2011

Coopers
Guinness archive fact sheet on cooperage www.guinness-storehouse.com/en/docs/Coopering_Process.pdf
Kilby, Kenneth *Coopers and Coopering*, Shire, 2004
Rootsweb page on coopers www.rootsweb.ancestry.com/~flbbm/heritage/cooper/barrelmaking.htm

Saddle and Harness Makers
Cawthorne, Nancy *George Emm & Son, Saddlers and Harness Makers of Paulton, Five Arches*, journal of Radstock, Midsomer Norton & District Museum Society, Issue 27
Requiem for a Saddler, Issue 68, Summer 2010

Stationers, Printers and Bookbinders
Dagnall, Harry *The Taxation of Paper in Great Britain 1643–1861: A History and Documentation*, BAPH, 1988
Duff, Gordon E. *A Century of the English Book Trade*, Bibliographical Society, 1905, printers, stationers and bookbinders from 1457 to 1557 online https://archive.org/details/centuryofenglish00duffuoft
Hills, Richard L. *Papermaking in Britain 1488–1988: A Short History*, Athlone, 1988

Packer, Maurice *Bookbinders of Victorian London*, British Library, 1991

Plomer, H.R. (England); Bushnell, G.H. (Scotland); McDix, E.R. (Ireland) *A Dictionary of printers and booksellers 1726–1775*, OUP, 1932

Plomer, Henry R. *Wills of English Printers and Stationers 1492–1630*, 1903

Ramsden, Charles *Bookbinders of the United Kingdom outside London, 1780–1840*, Batsford, 1954

Ramsden, Charles *London Bookbinders, 1780–1840*, Batsford, 1956

Wheelwrights, Carriage and Coachbuilders

Bampton, Daphne *Bamptons 1933–1979 A History in the Evolution of the Coachbuilding and Repairing Industry*, Bampton Bros, 1973

Burgess, James W. *A practical treatise on coach-building, historical and descriptive: containing full information on the various trades and processes involved, with hints on the proper keeping of carriages, &c*, Crosby, Lockwood and Co., London, 1881, **https://archive.org/details/ practicaltreatis00burg**

Georgano, Nick (Ed.) *The Beaulieu Encyclopedia of the Automobile: Coachbuilding*, Routledge, 2001

Mynard, Dennis C. *Salmons and Sons, The Tickford Coachbuilders*, Phillimore, 2007

Wood, Jonathan *Coachbuilding: The Hand-crafted Car Body*, Shire, 2008

INDEX